# MEMORIES OF THE BATTLE OF NEW ULM

Personal Accounts of the Sioux Uprising

L. A. Fritsche's *History of Brown County, Minnesota* (1916)

Edited by
*Don Heinrich Tolzmann*

HERITAGE BOOKS
2007

# HERITAGE BOOKS
*AN IMPRINT OF HERITAGE BOOKS, INC.*

**Books, CDs, and more—Worldwide**

For our listing of thousands of titles see our website
at
www.HeritageBooks.com

Published 2007 by
HERITAGE BOOKS, INC.
Publishing Division
65 East Main Street
Westminster, Maryland 21157-5026

Copyright © 2001 Don Heinrich Tolzmann

*Cover illustration courtesy of the
Brown County Historical Society, New Ulm, Minnesota*

All rights reserved. No part of this book may be reproduced or transmitted in any form or by any means, electronic or mechanical, including photocopying, recording or by any information storage and retrieval system without written permission from the author, except for the inclusion of brief quotations in a review.

International Standard Book Number: 978-0-7884-1863-7

# Table of Contents

Editor's Introduction ............................................. v

I. The Fritsche Family ........................................... 1
   1. About L. A. Fritsche ..................................... 3
   2. Reminiscences of the Indian War of 1862 ................ 11

II. The Uprising ................................................ 19
   3. Causes Leading to the Outbreak ......................... 21
   4. Complaints Against the Agents .......................... 23
   5. Schemes of the Traders ................................. 25
   6. The Indians' Protest ................................... 27
   7. Organization of Young Warriors ......................... 29
   8. First Act of Violence .................................. 31
   9. Pillaging Leads to Murder .............................. 35
   10. Tardy Action by the Government ........................ 39
   11. Beginning of the Massacre ............................. 41
   12. Other Bloody Deeds .................................... 43
   13. Captain Nix in Command ................................ 45
   14. Indians Besiege the Town .............................. 47
   15. A Fatal Ambush ........................................ 51
   16. Siege of New Ulm Continued ............................ 55
   17. Narrow Escape of Women and Children ................... 57
   18. Order Restored ........................................ 61

III. Personal Accounts .......................................... 63
   19. The Milford Massacre .................................. 65
   20. Cause of the Outbreak ................................. 67
   21. Vengeance on the Traders .............................. 71
   22. Settlers Taken by Surprise ............................ 75
   23. A Day of Terror ....................................... 77
   24. Theresa Henle's Account ............................... 81
   25. A Thrilling Experience ................................ 83
   26. Thrilling Incidents of the Battle of New Ulm .......... 87
   27. Reminiscences of the Little Crow Uprising ............. 91

IV. Punishment of the Sioux ............................... 103
    28. Introduction ........................................ 105
    29. Facts Concerning the Final Execution ................. 109
    30. The Execution ...................................... 113
    31. The Final Scene .................................... 115

V. Remembrance and Review ............................... 117
    32. Execution Site ...................................... 119
    33. Indian Massacre Monument ......................... 121
    34. The Milford Tablet ................................. 123
    35. The Monument .................................... 125
    36. As Viewed by Bishop Whipple ...................... 127
    37. Pensioners of the Sioux Uprising .................... 129

VI. Appendix ............................................. 131
    38. Establishment of Ft. Ridgely ........................ 133
    39. Siege of the Fort. ................................... 135
    40. Indian History and Treaties .......................... 151
    41. Pioneer Settlement .................................. 163
    42. The City of New Ulm .............................. 177

Editor's Conclusion ....................................... 185

Index ................................................... 187

# Editor's Introduction

New Ulm, Minnesota bore the brunt of the Sioux Uprising in 1862 during two battles, which decided the fate of what also became known as the Dakota Conflict. Had it not been brought to a halt there, there is no question that the conflagration would have spread throughout the Minnesota River Valley.[1]

As it played a pivotal role in the conflict, its perception and understanding of the events related to it are especially important. Indeed, New Ulm was obviously one of the key players, and was a central target in terms of military strategy. The best source of information regarding the German-American perspective of the uprising can be found within a county history, published by Dr. L.A. Fritsche in 1916, which contains a documentary history he edited of the conflict.[2] As this two-volume work has long been out of print, the editor has selected relevant sections dealing with the Dakota Conflict and edited them together to form a documentary history.

Of late a number of works have been published on the Dakota Conflict, but there is no work which presents and illuminates the history of the conflict from the point of view of New Ulm, again, a key player in the events of 1862.[3] To facilitate access to this history, the editor has

---

1 For a recent survey of the Dakota Conflict, see Duane Schultz, *Over the Earth I Come: The Great Sioux Uprising of 1862*. (New York: St. Martin's Press, 1992). This also includes a good selective bibliography of works dealing with the topic, pp. 291-97. Also, see: Michael Clodfelter, *The Dakota War: The United States Army Versus the Sioux, 1862-1865*. (Jefferson, North Carolina: McFarland & Co., 1998).

2 Dr. Fritsche's work was entitled: *History of Brown County, Minnesota: Its People, Industries and Institutions*. (Indianapolis: B.F. Bowen & Co., 1916), 2 vols. Although, of course, central to the history of the conflict, I have failed to find this work referenced in other works dealing with the uprising.

3 There are eyewitness accounts, which are cited in the works listed in footnote no. 5, but no attempt has been made at assembling a general survey as was the case with Fritsche's history. However, even here this was embedded within the framework of a larger general county history.

assembled this work by one of New Ulm's most prominent citizens, Dr. L.A. Fritsche.

Dr. Fritsche was born May 28, 1862 in Lafayette Township, Nicollet County, and was the son of some of the earliest settlers of the area. At the time of the uprising he was less than three months old. He spent his boyhood on the farm, attended St. Peter High School, entered the University of Michigan at Ann Arbor, and graduated from the medical college in 1887. Returning to New Ulm, he practiced medicine, and then went to Germany for a postgraduate course at the University of Berlin, which he completed in 1890.

In the state of Minnesota he rose to prominence in his profession, becoming a member of the State Board of Medical Examiners in 1900, and served as a brigade surgeon in the National Guard from 1910 to 1916; he also was sworn into federal service during the time of the Mexican border troubles. In 1910, he was first elected mayor of New Ulm, and served a total of ten years in that position. He also had served since the 1890s in a number of positions in the City of New Ulm, as well as Brown County.

Fritsche also played an important role as a German-American community leader in the state of Minnesota. He was one of the organizers of the farmer-labor party in New Ulm, and was candidate for governor in the primary elections in 1924 and 1928, and was candidate of his party for congress in 1930. In 1922, he entered the race for the farmer-labor nomination for the U.S. Senate. During the anti-German hysteria of World War I, he and other officials of New Ulm and Brown County were removed from office by the Minnesota Commission of Public Safety. At the time of his death in 1931, he was considered "one of the foremost citizens" of the state of Minnesota.[4] His history of Brown County, published in 1916, is considered the standard history of the area.

Drawn from Dr. Fritsche's county history, this work is of value, not only as it provides a documentary history of the conflict, but because it contributes to an understanding of how New Ulmers viewed and

---

4 See "Dr. L.A. Fritsche Called by Death," *New Ulm Journal*, (19 June 1931).

understood the conflict. Although they clearly condemned the mistreatment of the Sioux, which led to the uprising, they at the same time condemned the death and destruction that followed. This in itself provides insight into the dilemma and tragedy of the situation.

As Fritsche's history has long been out of print, and no other comparable general history has appeared, it is appropriate to compile and edit this work based on Fritsche's county history, especially in view of several anniversaries, including the 140th anniversary of the Dakota Conflict in 2002, and the 150th anniversary of the founding of New Ulm in 2004.

I would especially like to express gratitude to Dr. Theodore Fritsche, the son of Dr. Fritsche, who presented me with a copy of his father's history. Having published two works relating to New Ulm history, it readily became apparent to me that the materials dealing with the conflict formed a narrative that was worthy of being edited together as a whole.[5]

As a German-American historian, I have taken an interest in New Ulm because of family relations in and around the town. In 1870, my great-grandfather's family moved to a farm northwest of New Ulm from German Lake, Minnesota. They moved to a farm, that had belonged to the Schwandt family, which had been almost totally wiped out during the uprising.

The Rev. Alexander Berghold of New Ulm provides us with a striking description of what neighbors found when they came to the farm and what been done to the family:

> Schwandt's son-in-law was lying on the door steps with three bullets in his body. His wife (Schwandt's daughter), who had been with child, was found dead, her womb cut open and the unborn child nailed to a tree. Her brother, a thirteen-year-old lad, whom

---

5 See Don Heinrich Tolzmann, ed., *The Sioux Uprising in Minnesota, 1862: Jacob Nix's Eyewitness History*. (Indianapolis: Max Kade German-American Center, Indiana University-Indianapolis & Indiana German Heritage Society, 1994; and also: Don Heinrich Tolzmann, ed., *New Ulm in Word and Picture: J.H. Strasser's History of a German-American Settlement, 1892*. (Indiana: Max Kade German-American Center, Indiana University-Indianapolis & Indianapolis German Heritage Society, 1997).

the Indians had thought they had killed, saw how the child was taken alive from the womb of his sister, and nailed to the tree, where it lived for a little while. This terrible deed was done in the forenoon of August the 18$^{th}$. The mother was found in the field beheaded. Beside her lay the body of their hired man, Frass. Towards the evening, the boy regained a little strength and fled into the next settlement, a distance of three miles. He entered Bushe's house only to find some thirty corpses, among them a three-year-old child, wounded, and sitting beside its dead mother. The boy took the child with him, carried it about four miles, and being unable to take it farther, left it at a house, promising to return the next morning. He did this in order to be able to save himself. He made good his escape to Fort Ridgely, traveling for four nights, and hiding the day. The child was afterwards found in captivity among the Indians, and was brought to Fort Ridgely, where it died from the effects of its wounds and exposure. [6]

The boy's only surviving sister, Mary Schwandt, who was kidnaped and raped, later wrote a well-known account of her ordeal, which she referred to as "the incidents of that dreadful night and the four following dreadful days" of her captivity, and commented that: "While in Little Crow's village I saw some of my father's cattle and many of our household goods in the hands of the Indians. I now knew that my family had been plundered, and I believed murdered." She went on to say:

> I was very, very wretched, and cared not how soon I too was killed . . . my eyes were always red and swollen from constant weeping . . . But soon there came a time when I did not weep. I could not. The dreadful scenes I had witnessed, the suffering that I had undergone, the almost certainty that my family had all been killed, and that I was alone in the world, and the belief that I was destined to witness other things as horrible as those I had seen, and that my career of suffering and misery had only begun, all came to my comprehension, and when I realized my utterly wretched, helpless and hopeless situation, for I did not think I would ever be

---

6 Cited in: Tolzmann, *The Sioux Uprising*, xxi.

released, I became as one paralyzed and could hardly speak... and went about like a sleepwalker.[7]

On 18 August 1915, the State of Minnesota erected the Schwandt Monument in front of my great-grandfather's farm in honor of those who had perished there on 18 August 1862: Johan and Christina Schwandt, and their children, Frederick and Christina: John and Karoline Schwandt Walz; and John Frass. It stands there as a silent memorial to what had taken place more than half a century before.[8]

Given this family background, I, obviously grew up interested in the history of New Ulm, the uprising, the pioneers, etc., and, have published works dealing with these topics. My intention in editing this work for publication was to make the information buried in Fritsche's history available, and to provide access to the valuable source information it contained with regard to the battle for New Ulm.

In part one of this work, the 1916 biography of Fritsche is found, together with the recollection of his father regarding the uprising. Thereafter, Fritsche provides information on the uprising, as well as personal accounts thereof, in parts two and three. Part four deals with the punishments rendered as a result of the conflict, which is followed by several sections on how the uprising was dealt with in terms of historical remembrance. The appendices provide information on Fort Ridgely, the treaties with the Indians, the pioneers, and the City of New Ulm. The editor closes with some final comments on the work in historical context. Finally, special thanks to Dorothy Young, Germanic Languages and Literatures, University of Cincinnati, for her assistance in the preparation of this manuscript.

DHT

---

7 Ibid, pp.xxi-xxii.

8 Ibid, pp.xvii-xviii.

# I. The Fritsche Family

# 1. About L. A. Fritsche

Louis Albert Fritsche was born on May 28, 1862, on his father's homestead in Lafayette, Nicollet County, within two miles of the city of New Ulm.

His paternal grandfather, John Karl Fritsche, with a family of eight children, emigrated to this country from Saxony, Germany, in the year 1854, and landed at New York on May 22. On account of the unsettled political conditions in Germany following the revolution of 1848 and, in order to have his sons escape the military service, he decided to seek his fortune in the New World. The voyage was made in a three-masted sailing vessel, named the *Leibnitz* and took fifty-two days to cross the ocean. The voyage was a very tedious and boisterous one. His destination was Chicago and reached that city in due time. He resided there for one year. Having been a small farmer in Saxony, he longed to once more to engage in agriculture. About this time the German Land Association of Chicago was being organized for the purpose of establishing a colony in some territory, which was being opened up for settlement in the Northwest. He became a member of this association.

The choice of location for this settlement fell upon the present site of this city and country surrounding it. The association acquired three hundred and twenty acres from the government, which was platted in city lots. John Karl Fritsche pre-empted a homestead of one hundred and sixty acres joining the city site in the summer of 1855. In the following year a colony from Cincinnati bought up the charter of the German Land Association and in addition acquired John Karl Fritsche's homestead, together with thirteen other homestead quarters, and had the same platted into lots. This merger made the city site exceptionally large.

Frederick Fritsche, the second son of John Karl Fritsche, and the father of the subject of this biography, upon reaching his majority, pre-empted a homestead of one hundred and sixty acres in the year 1860 on the north side of the Minnesota River, in Nicollet County, two miles from New Ulm. This homestead later became the nucleus of a large stock farm.

The maternal grandfather, Christian Lillie, emigrated with a family of four children from Hanover, Germany, to this country in the year of 1852 and first settled in Allegheny County, New York. There he resided until the year of 1858, when he removed to the state of Minnesota and pre-empted a claim in Nicollet County, four miles distant from New Ulm.

Frederick Fritsche was married to Louise Lillie, youngest daughter of Christian Lillie, on April 20, 1861. Eight children were born to this union, namely: Louis Albert, Bertha, Emil H., Fred W., Otto A., Rudolph E., Carl J. and Henry W. Bertha was married to William H. Mueller, of St. Peter, who is a member of the manufacturing firm of Johnson & Company. Emil H. and Otto A. have remained on the divided homestead and are prosperous farmers. Fred W. practiced dental surgery until his death, three years ago. Rudolph E. was a member of the hardware firm of Arnold & Fritsche and died five years ago. Carl J. and Henry W. died during childhood.

Louis Albert was raised as all junior pioneers and shared all the pleasures, as well as all of the privations and tribulations, which are incident to pioneer and order life. At the time of the Sioux uprising he was three months old, and was the cause of much anxiety for his mother. Before the outbreak the Indians would camp in the Fritsche ravine every winter, near the Fritsche log cabin, and when the pale-face baby was born the squaws would often come in to fondle the same.

At the age of six years, Louis Fritsche was sent to the district school, which was a small log building, and two miles distant. At that time there were no graded public roads, only beaten tracks winding over the hill, through timber and prairie, lined on both sides with high buffalo grass. At the age of ten years his fortune changed, so far as his education was concerned. His father, Frederick Fritsche, was elected treasurer of Nicollet County in 1872, and re-elected four times thereafter. The family removed to the county seat at St. Peter and, thereby, the children were given a better opportunity for an education, as St. Peter at that time had good graded schools and a high school. This was a stepping stone to his future career.

In the year of 1878 the family moved back to the farm, as his father was wanting to retire from office and actively re-engage in the raising of blooded stock. The management of the farm was placed in Louis Albert's management until 1882, when his father retired from office to reassume the management.

The following year, Louis Albert, after attaining his majority, procured a second-grade teacher's certificate and taught district school for one year.

Having met with the requirement of the law at that time, necessitating one year of experience as a teacher, before a first grade certificate could be granted, he procured a first grade teacher's certificate from both Nicollet and Brown Counties.

However, he did not follow teaching any more, as he wanted another means of making a livelihood. With the above mentioned credentials he entered the medical department of the University of Michigan on September 24, 1884. While a student at Ann Arbor he was an honorary member of the Adelphia Literary Society.

After completing the full course of three years he graduated from that institution on June 30, 1887. The day after his graduation, on July 1, 1887, the new medical law of the state of Minnesota went into effect, which required all practitioners to pass a state examination. The first examination of the newly created medical board was held at the state capitol in St. Paul on July 5 and 6, 1887, and only three applicants were present. Doctor Fritsche passed this examination without any difficulty and was awarded license no. 1, and therefore, has the distinction of having received the first license issued by the state board of medical examiners of this state.

On August 1, 1887, he opened an office in New Ulm and practiced there until the latter part of April, 1889. Then he went to Berlin, Germany, to do post-graduate work and specialize in surgery at that famous university. At the same time he intended to take his second doctor's degree. At the end of two semesters he passed the "examen rigorosum, tentamen medicum" and presented a thesis for graduation. On March 31, 1890, he had the degree of doctor of Medicine and Surgery conferred upon him with the standing of cum laude, from that university. During the third semester, from April 1 to August 1, he was second assistant to the famous surgeon, Prof. Dr. Julius Wolff.

He was a member of the Tenth International Medical Congress which convened in Berlin from the 6th to the 13th of August, 1890, and had the honor to present two cases in the English language to the Gynecological Section for Prof. Dr. Alfred Duhrssen. This congress was attended by seven thousand professors and doctors from all over the world.

Doctor Fritsche returned home October 15, the same fall and re-opened his office, and has been in active practice up to the present time. The doctor is a member of the Brown County Medical Society, the Southern Minnesota Medical Association, the State Medical Association and the American Medical Association. When the Minnesota Medical Society was united with the Southern Minnesota Medical Association, four years ago, he was elected the first president of the new organization.

Medical career: He has served as health officer of the city of New Ulm from 1891 to 1894. He served as a member of the pension medical examining board under President Cleveland's second administration for this district. He was elected as coroner of Brown County for four terms, serving from 1896 to 1904. In the year 1900 he was appointed as a member of the state board of medical examiners by Gov. John Lind for three years, and the last of which he was the president of the board. He is surgeon to the Loretto and Union hospitals of New Ulm.

Civil career: He was elected a member of the board of education for three years and served from 1893 to 1896. He was appointed as a member of the board of public works by Mayor Weschke in 1904 and served as such until 1912. In 1912 he was elected mayor of the city and has been twice re-elected without opposition, and still serves in this capacity.

Military career: In the year of 1907, Gov. John A. Johnson commissioned him as a member of Brig. Gen Joseph Bobleter's staff as brigade surgeon with the rank of major. This commission was renewed by Gov. A. O. Eberhart, and after General Bobleter's death, was continued on the staff of General Reeves and again by his successor, Gen. A. W. Wright.

Business career: In the year 1900 he was elected as president of the Brown County Bank and has served as such only in an honorary capacity up to the present time. He is vice-president of the New Ulm Roller Milling Company and a director in several other industrial enterprises. He is also director and medical director of the Minnesota Commercial Men's Association, of Minneapolis, which is a mutual health and accident insurance company for business and traveling salesmen.

Political affiliation: He has always been a Democrat in politics and attended many Democratic state conventions as a delegate. In the year of 1908 he was elected as a delegate from the second congressional district to the Democratic National Convention at Denver. He was interested in the candidacy of Gov. John A. Johnson for the presidential nomination, as the governor had been a schoolmate and life-long friend of his.

In July, 1914, the doctor received an invitation to join a commission of mayors and civic leaders, headed by United States Senator Duncan Fletcher, from Florida, to attend an International Congress of Municipal Executives held at London, to attend the International Urban Exposition at Lyons, France, and to visit a number of European cities for study purposes. The commission sailed from New York on July 9 and met with some thrilling experiences before they returned home. Each member of the commission was provided with a personal letter of introduction from former secretary of state William Jennings Bryan, to all of our ambassadors and consular agents abroad, who were apprised of the coming of this commission by Mr. Bryan. A hearty welcome awaited them at Liverpool and London and the lord mayors of these cities entertained this party at tea in their respective mansion houses.

The International Municipal Congress was opened on Monday noon, July 20, by Viscount Peel, chairman, in the presence of our ambassador, Mr. Page. Other speakers were the Earl of Kintore, Lord Rotherham, Sir John A. Cockburn and Senator Fletcher.

The afternoon session was called at three o'clock, under the chairmanship of Senator Fletcher, and this session was devoted to public health administration and sanitation. The first address was courteously left to the Americans and was delivered by Dr. L. A. Fritsche, from Minnesota.

The commission left London on Saturday morning, July 25, and reached Paris the same evening. At the Paris station they were met by Mr. Sulzdorf, the secretary to our ambassador, Mr. Herrick, and escorted to the hotel.

Monday afternoon this commission was tendered a reception by the governor and city officials of Paris, our ambassador, Mr. Herrick, being present. Tuesday afternoon Mr. Herrick tendered the party a reception, to which the city officials of Paris were invited in return. During this reception, about 5:30 o'clock, a telegram came in announcing that Austria had declared war against Serbia. The countenances of the Pairs officials dropped at once and one could notice that this telegram was an evil foreboding for them. That same evening an immense demonstration of tens of thousands of people took place, crying "Down with the war, we want no war," but this demonstration was gradually controlled by the police.

On Wednesday evening, July 29, the commission left for Lyons, reaching that city late in the night. A most cordial reception awaited them there. The first thing they saw the next morning were the runs on the large banks. Thousands of people had lined up in front of the banks to draw out their deposits. The next day the banks refused to pay out any more money, and it went hard with the Americans, as their traveling checks were not accepted any more. The war clouds were getting darker and the *esprit de corps* of the party was being gradually dampened. On Friday evening, July 31, Mayor Herriott, of Lyons, tendered the commission a reception on the exposition grounds and this was the last official function. After returning to the hotel that evening, a hasty war council was held by the party and it was decided to discontinue the journey. On Saturday morning train service was already interrupted on account of the heavy movement of troops to the Alsatian border, and the balance of the commission had considerable difficulty in making their way back to Paris.

Doctor Fritsche, with two members of the commission, decided to go to Switzerland and left Lyons on the last train out to Geneva. Upon reaching Geneva on Saturday evening they learned that Germany had declared war against Russia. On Sunday morning all train service to the border countries had been suspended, and the Doctor, with thousands of American tourists, was bottled up in Switzerland for three weeks. After all of the armies of the belligerent countries had been moved to the various war fronts, railroad transportation was restored in a measure, and the doctor was enabled to cross the Swiss border into Germany. While on the way to Frankfurt on the Main he passed two train loads of wounded soldiers, one was carrying wounded Frenchmen and the other wounded Germans–a sight that will never be forgotten. After making short visits in Frankfurt on the Main, Berlin, Frankfurt on the Oder, Leipzig and Jena, visiting the hospitals where the wounded soldiers were cared for, he was fortunate enough to engage his return passage on a Holland liner from Rotterdam. When in sight of the statue of the "Goddess of Liberty" in New York Harbor, sixteen hundred passengers breathed a sign of relief and thanked heaven that they had escaped from that European turmoil.

Doctor Fritsche was married in Berlin, Germany, June 14, 1890, to Amalie Pfaender, daughter of Col. William Pfaender, deceased, who served in the Union Army during the Civil War, and who later had charge of Ft. Ridgely from the year of 1862 to 1866. Seven children have been born to Doctor and Mrs. Fritsche, namely: Elsa, who graduated from the University of Minnesota in June, 1915, and is now engaged in teaching at Dover, of this state; Albert, who is a medical student in the University of Minnesota; William, who is a medical student at Marquette University of Milwaukee; Louise, who is a pupil of the New Ulm high school; Carl and Theodore, who are pupils in the graded schools, and Alexander Frederick, who died at the age of seven months.

As a junior pioneer, Doctor Fritsche has beheld the transformation that followed the advent of the white man in this part of the country—the reclamation from a wilderness in the life-time of hundreds of those who assisted in the onerous tasks of wresting from the idle and indolent savage, as fair land as the sun ever shone on, molded now into the magnificent commonwealth of Minnesota, whit its cities and towns, its schools and churches, its network of railroads, its thousands of rural homes, many of them modern in all respects and connected with one another by the telephones, its vast herds that have displaced the buffalo and the antelope, and its golden fields—a great state subdued, beautified and made rich from the fertility of its own matchless soil. What a privilege to have witnessed such a transformation, inconceivable in any but this wonderful country, for such a transition one could not witness on the continent of Europe were he permitted to live a thousand years.

Blessed is the memory when the early settlers ranged with a free hand in the work of reclamation, amid scenes forever vanished, or now obscured by the stage-settings of civilization. Sixty-two years ago, so far as the works of man were concerned, all was desolation. Buffalo and antelope scurried over the great, wild pastures in herds and bands innumerable, while the Indian, in all his pride and glory, roamed as the undisputed master of the region that to man was merely a solitude of limitless possibilities.

## 2. Reminiscences of the Indian War of 1862

### Frederick Fritsche[9]

On the 18th of August, 1862, when we were stacking grain on the farm in Lafayette, the rumor came that the Sioux Indians had broken their peace and were killing all the white people they could get hold of. As I had a good deal of the time for seven years in Minnesota been among those Indians and had the impression that they were good people, I did not believe that they would do that; so I did not pay any attention to such rumors. But the same evening after dark, Athanasius Henle and Alois Palmer passed our place headed for New Ulm with a wagon-load of wounded and murdered children, which of course convinced me that there was a general uprising of the Indians Mr. Henle and Mr. Palmer were so kind as to take my wife and baby along and I followed them later in the night to New Ulm. At New Ulm a great many killed and wounded people had been brought in there and there was much excitement. People were preparing ammunition, fixing up all kinds of arms, building stacked breastworks, and preparing for war generally. Tuesday morning, August 19, all able-bodied men organized into companies. We farmers from the Nicollet County side organized the Lafayette company. Fidel Diepolder was elected lieutenant and F. Fritsche and Mathias Lump were chosen corporals of the company. Farmers from all directions were coming into New Ulm, as the news of the uprising of the Indians had spread all over the country. Nothing unusual happened in the forenoon of the 19th of August. People someway felt tired already, laying around and doing nothing, and some of the farmers who has left their places the night before in great haste made up their minds to go back again and look after stock, etc. Some eight or ten from up the Cottonwood River, toward Leavenworth, started out with one or two-horse teams, as some people had an idea that the Indians would not attack New Ulm at all. But early in the afternoon we found that we were badly mistaken. The Indians unexpectedly attacked the town. When the firing began great confusion of the people took place. Instead of women and

---

9 These reminiscences were published in the *New Ulm News* in September, 1909. At the time of the massacre Mr. Fritsche resided near Lafayette, Nicollet county, and took part in that never-to-be-forgotten struggle with the savage Sioux. He now resides in New Ulm, advanced in years, but still possessed of all of his faculties.

children staying inside of the houses, a great many came out on the street, looking and crying for their relatives. The first one killed was a twelve-year-old girl, the only child of Mr. And Mrs. Pauli. Shortly before some Indians had been seen about one file south of town, chasing some farmers. At once Captain Nix, who was in command of all the forces, detailed a party of twelve or fifteen men to go in that direction. But when they got there the Indians were gone. In the meantime, the Indians attacked New Ulm, and so these men returned double-quick to town. They had hardly managed to get through the Indian fire line when they had one man killed and a few were slightly wounded before they got into town.

In a very short time New Ulm was surrounded by the red devils and the bullets came in from all directions, but most of the shooting was too high. However, no objection to that was made on our side. After a couple of hours of fighting we felt satisfied that we were the masters of the situation; at least we thought so. But just then came the trying time–the cry of "fire!" The red-skins had begun to fire the town. Four houses were on fire at once, on the corner of Broadway and North Third streets. They were the houses of Fred Rehfeld, P. Kropper and Steinhauser on fire. Not far from there toward the center of the town, the houses were filled up with women, children and old people. The situation looked hopelessly dangerous. But at the critical time came up John Hauenstein, Charles Wagner and August Hellmann, with the cry, "Come on, boys." Julius Guetling, John Peller, August Riemer, F. Fritsche and August Westphal followed. A party of eight men only started toward the burning buildings.

The Indians had a strong position near the fires. Up along the hill on the west side of New Ulm, on what is now State Street, a short distance south of the Methodist church, the Indians had posted themselves behind a small hill, so we could hardly see any of them. From there on our left side and in front of us they opened a murderous fire on our few men. At the same time a detachment of John Bellm's company were in possession of the Schalk building now the Buenger block on Minnesota Street, and they opened fire on the Indians, which helped to check their advance toward the center of the town. This prevented their firing any more buildings in that locality. Great danger was evident at that time, as the wind was blowing toward the center of the town. We lost four men out of eight by that attack. We had one killed and three wounded. August Riemer, killed; Julius

Guetling, John Peller and August Westphal, wounded.. The Indians kept up a lively fire from the hill on the west, so Captain Jacob Nix ordered a few men to take possession of the Forster building on Broadway, and they kept the Indians in check from that direction. While all this fighting was going on, black clouds came up from the west and northwest, and in a short time a thunder shower broke loose, which sounded just as though artillery from heaven had mixed in with our firing. Then it commenced to rain and the water poured down in streams. As the heavy rain soaked buildings, haystacks and all else with water, the Indians ceased setting fires to the buildings, ammunition got wet, and firing stopped on both sides. The Indians gradually disappeared toward the west, which gave us a long-needed rest. But soon afterward firing was heard from the west and a few minutes later a horse team dashed down the hill without a driver, which was soon followed with the news that eight or ten men had been killed about a mile west of town, while coming back from a patrolling expedition. There was a party of men sent to the bloody scene, and the dead and wounded were brought to town. When all this excitement was over we calculated to look for our dear ones, good news came from St. Peter. About ten or twelve courageous mounted men came from there to the assistance of New Ulm, and promised that some more would come as soon as possible. Certainly these men were greeted with warm cheers. They were given quarters for their animals, and a good supper provided for them–the best that could be cone under the circumstances. But sorry to say that some of them went back to St. Peter that night.

NERVOUS PICKETS

When getting dark I was called upon to do picket duty along State Street, on the hill west of town. Being rather thinly clad and wet from the rain, I felt cold, for it was a cool, damp night, and as I did not have any supper in the evening, it made it very disagreeable to stay there until morning. By daybreak we noticed some moving objects at a distance west of us, but it was too dark yet to plainly see what they were. So we kept watching carefully, and by and by the objects came toward us, very slowly though. The men to my right were getting excited, and one of them spoke out rather plainly, "Indians," when they at once ran into town. As the supposed Indians came near enough to be seen plainly, they proved to be a herd of cattle. Those men who left their places were all strangers to us.

On my left side were some brave men from Cottonwood township. I remember Theodore Reim as one of them, and as we had been in the fight the day before were not quite so easily scared.

Wednesday, August 20, 1862, Charles E. Flandrau was put in command of all the forces. During the night help had come in from different places. One company from St. Peter, Capt. Charles E. Flandrau,; one company from Mankato, Captain Bierbauer; and later in the day came two companies from LeSueur, one under Capt. E. C. Saunders. Capt. Jacob Nix was considering to send a letter up to Ft. Ridgely to Sergeant Jones, asking for some pieces of artillery and ammunition. But the question was who should go that eighteen miles, and most likely with Indians all around. The right man was already on hand. It was Xavier Zollner, then a young man, who having heard the conversation, came up and said he would go if given a good horse. He got the horse and letter and off he went. He reached Ft. Ridgely safe and sound, and although he had seen Indians at different places on his way, his good horse got him through. After he got inside the fort the Indians surrounded it. He took part in the fight there and the next day he came back to New Ulm, bringing an answer from Sergeant Jones that the artillery would be furnished if there were men to take it through. Xavier Zollner is now over seventy years old, and is living on his nice farm in West Newton, near St. George, Nicollet County. He is hale and hearty yet.

During the flight on Tuesday, August 19, good service was done by the rifle section of sharp-shooters of the Turner Society. These men had good rifles and made effective use of them. Many other men also did good work. In fact everybody I noticed did their duty the best they could. On Thursday and Friday, the 21st and 22nd of August, we were patrolling the Nicollet County side of the river, to look after helpless or wounded people, and in the evenings reported our doings and observations to commander Flandrau. We did not see any Indians, nor did we find any traces of them. But Saturday morning the 23rd, smoke and fires could be seen from New Ulm in different directions in the country. Farm buildings were being burned, a sure sign that the Indians were coming nearer. Another attack was expected. It looked as though these fires were the signals for them, as they were kept up nearly alike and were advancing at about the same speed on both sides of the Minnesota River toward New Ulm.

On Saturday morning, to our surprise, the Lafayette company was ordered to join Capt. William Huey's company of St. Peter, to march to the Nicollet County side of the river, and at the same time protect the ferry near the Globe Mills. Of the Lafayette company most of the men were on picket duty, so we were only about nine or ten men to join Captain Huey's company. We followed in disgust, especially as our families and loved ones were all in New Ulm, and an attack was feared. We crossed the river on the ferry, marched across the bottom land to the bluffs, on the Nicollet county side. We kept on going north about a distance of two miles from new Ulm in the neighborhood of August Rutenberg's and Adolph Schilling's farms. There we saw seven Indians on horseback going toward Henry Wellner's place. A few of Captain Huey's men unexpectedly to us, fired at these Indians, more than one-half of a mile off. Then the Indians noticed us; they stopped, and before our eyes they set fire to Mr. Wellner's hay stacks and buildings. After the fire had a good start they galloped off north, toward the Ft. Ridgely road.

### CUT OFF FROM THE TOWN

About the same time we could hear some lively shooting going on in New Ulm. A few of our Lafayette men went to Captain Huey and told him that we feared New Ulm was attached by the Redskins, and we thought it advisable to return to New Ulm, as we had our families there. But the captain did not think so. He said most likely some men who had been on guard last night discharged to clear their guns and there was no danger. After a while the captain admitted that New Ulm was attacked, and gave command to return to New Ulm. When we came to the bluff on Henry Mueller's place, his house was on fire, but no Indians were to be seen. We then marched toward town. As we came near the ferry the Indians from all directions came to the ferry on the New Ulm side to meet us. A great many Indians took possession of the Globe Mills. They opened a lively fire towards us, but without any effect at the time. It was a flat, level place, without any protection or shelter where they came to a stand, so it might become dangerous, and the air was filled with bullets. As we were acquainted there, we told the captain to take possession of a timber lot nearby, which he thought was a good idea, and he called the men up and told them about it. The timber lot was along the river bank, on the right side of the road to the ferry. On the left side and surrounding there was a flat meadow and no trees. We took the road to the ferry. Captain Huey in front, and the rest of the men followed. As we came near the ferry on the river bank, we turned to the right in the timber grove. There were trees three or four feet in diameter, which no Indian bullet could get through. When we took the road toward the ferry the Indians ceased firing. Probably they expected us to enter the ferry boat; then they would have killed the most of us. We surprised them. Now fire was opened on both sides, and we heard the bullets rattle in the trees as thick as hail. One man from St. Peter by the name of Summers, who wore a white shirt, was shot through the lower body, and was severely wounded. A few other men were slightly wounded, and that is all we had to suffer there. After fighting there for some time the command came to leave the place to go to St. Peter. The reason why, we could not find out. Some of the St. Peter men had the idea the Indians might attack St. Peter, and they had better start for that place. This was a hard blow for us Lafayette men, but as we were only about ten men we had to follow. It was almost unbearable to have our families in New Ulm, and we were only about six or eight blocks from them and yet could not protect them. Of course we had the river between us, and the ferry rope was cut off. H. H. Beussman and I considered different plans, but could not do anything. Our ammunition was nearly used up and we had not a bite to eat all day; we were tired and exhausted, as for nearly a week we had hardly any sleep at all and scarcely enough to eat. We followed the procession because we had to. When we came on top of the hill on the Nicollet County side we could overlook New Ulm. We say nothing but fire and smoke, and heard no end of shooting and firing guns. And our families and relatives and dear ones were all imprisoned there. Well, we thought that is the last of them. We will never see them again, not even the ashes. We were not a half mile from our fighting ground when both mills–the Eagle and Globe–were on fire; also the houses in that part of town–all went up in smoke. We would ten times sooner have faced bullets of the enemies than to see our families and friends surrounded by fire and smoke and savage Indians, and not be able to help them.

We marched toward St. Peter, and when we came to Nicollet Creek we met Capt. E. St. Julien Cox and a company of about one hundred men, fairly well armed, headed to New Ulm. We Lafayette men turned right round and joined Cox's men and were ready to go to New Ulm. As we felt quite hungry we helped ourselves to Captain Cox's provisions. We asked

Cox to go right on the New Ulm, as help was needed there. All his men were ready to go, but as night came on he ordered us to camp at the old Joel Kennedy place, about fourteen miles from New Ulm. During the night we could see the fire in New Ulm, and we feared the last houses were burning. The next morning we marched to New Ulm, and reached there about noon. At Redstone the ferry rope was cut and the ferry was on the other side. But soon the ferry was in order and crossing began. When the first men came to the other side they found an Indian pony with saddle and bridle on. They brought the pony across the river and Captain Cox mounted it. He rode that pony into New Ulm and was proud of it. At New Ulm we learned that the Indians made their last attack that morning and had quit fighting before we came. About five blocks were left standing in the center of the town. We were happy to find our families all alive, as the Indians did not get a chance to murder women and children. But there was great suffering with some of them. They had been confined in the houses day and night. I do not recollect the number of men killed and wounded during the fight, but many a friend was missing. Provisions and ammunition were getting scarce in New Ulm, so it was decided to move the families to St. Peter. It took us two days, via Mankato, to reach that town, and we used mostly ox-teams. It was reported that General Sibley with a regiment of soldiers had marched to Ft. Ridgely and more troops were following, and it was thought that the Indians could be driven away. We farmers, therefore, returned to our farms, and left the families in St. Peter. A small band of Indians made their appearance at Cottonwood and Cambria, and killed a few more men. But they were driven away instantly, as everybody was armed and no mercy was allowed.

# II. The Uprising

## 3. Causes Leading to the Outbreak[10]

The chief cause of the Indian outbreak of 1862 was the dishonesty of the "Indian Agents" sent out by the government to look after the disbursements of funds due the Indians, who, in many cases, worked in connection with the traders at the posts or agencies, to greatly defraud the Indian. While the general government usually sought to live up to its treaties, it was thwarted in its attempt to fulfill its treaty promises by its agents.

In 1858 the government purchased that portion of the reservation lying north of the Minnesota River, so that the Indians retained only a strip of land ten miles wide and one hundred and fifty miles long. For the portion thus ceded, costing the government about one cent an acre, two hundred and seventy-five thousand dollars were to be paid annually to the chiefs of the Sissetons and Waphetons, and also thirty thousand dollars for the education of their tribes. The Medawakontons and Wahpekutas were also to receive two hundred thousand dollars annually, payable to their chiefs, and thirty thousand dollars for their education, the government promising the Indians at that time, to do all in its power for their education, elevation and civilization. The whole sum was to be paid annually for fifty years; about five hundred and fifty-five thousand dollars.

This honest debt contracted by the government, was, with the exception of an insignificant portion of it, never paid; and this was the principal cause of the dissatisfaction and revolt of the Indians. The government did, indeed, pay the stipulated sum regularly, but the superintendents, agents, etc., to whom the money was entrusted for distribution and payment, managed to keep the greater portion of it for themselves.

The following extracts, which, alas, contain neither slander nor exaggeration, nor misrepresentation of the real facts will give the reader an idea of how the Indians were treated. A prominent officer, Major Kitzing Pritchette, being sent from Washington to investigate the numerous

---

10 The following account of the New Ulm massacre and the causes leading up to that event is taken from the writings of Rev. Alexander Berghold, who was the organizer of the first Catholic church in Brown County.

complaints of gigantic swindles raised by the Indians, in his official report says:

"The complaints which are made at all their meetings refer to the imperfect fulfillment or non-compliance with the conditions of the treaty."

Tag-ma-na, a chief of the assembled Indians, said in his presence:

"The Indians sold their land in Traverse des Sioux. I say what they tell us. For fifty years we were to receive fifty thousand dollars annually, and we were promised three hundred thousand dollars. We have seen nothing of it."

At the same meeting, Mahpya Wicasta (Man-of-the-Cloud), the second chief of the assembled Indians, said:

"In the Treaty of Traverse de Sioux we were to receive two hundred and seventy-five thousand dollars as soon as we had entered upon the land pointed out by the government. Tell us what was done with it? Every paleface knows that we are for the past five years on the territory named in the treaty, and as yet we have received none of the money."

A principal cause of these swindles were the acts of the so-called traders, who were consequently also the cause of the dissatisfaction of the Indians. These traders were merchants licensed to sell goods to the Indians, or to trade with them. Since, as a rule, the Indians had no money to pay for goods they bought, the trader would bring his bills to the paymaster at the time payment was to be made to the Indians, if such a time ever came, and the Indians, being neither able to read or write, these bills were shamefully and unmercifully changed and increased. The sums thus deducted from the amounts due the Indians was a transaction as cruel as it was unjust, but the poor red man was helpless. His complaint could be lodged only through an interpreter, who, although under oath, managed through the powerful influence of the traders to conceal the truth as much as possible. Others, though commanding both languages, were not listened to by the agents. The Indians were often so much cheated that they had as little pay after a payment which would amount to hundreds of thousands of dollars, as they had before.

## 4. Complaints Against the Agents

Judge Young, sent from Washington to investigate the complaints against Alexander Ramsey, at that time superintendent of Indian affairs, and later governor of Minnesota, says in his report:

"Alexander Ramsey was principally accused of having in spite of the protests of the Indians, in violation of the laws of the treaties, and in utter disregard of the solemn promises upon the part of the government, paid the greater portion of the money to a man named Hugh Tyler for payment or distribution among the Indians or half-breeds. According to the treaties the money was to be paid to the chiefs."

And thus of the two hundred and seventy-five thousand dollars which should have been paid to the Indians, according to Article IV of the Treaty of Traverse de Sioux, Ramsey gave two hundred and fifty thousand to Hugh Tyler under the pretext that the money belonged to traders and half-breeds. Mr. Tyler also received seventy thousand of the one hundred and ten thousand dollars, which, according to the treaty of August 5, 1851, should have been paid to the Medawakontons. altogether, of the three hundred and eighty-five thousand dollars belonging to the Indians, Tyler received three hundred and twenty thousand as a recompense for his labors in the Senate in behalf of the treaties, and also to reimburse him for his expenses in securing the consent of the chiefs. Such were his claims.

During the year 1857 a number of Indians were induced by a trader to sign a paper, the object of which, he said, was to cause a portion of the money they owed to the traders to be returned to them. But it was in reality a simple order in his favor, and the Indians were again cheated out of twelve thousand dollars. Wherever there was stealing the Indians had to pay for it, the amount being simply deducted from money due them.

But the officers appointed by the government to deal with the Indians managed to secure the benefits of the treaties for themselves. From the first to the last they were united for the one purpose of deceiving the Indians. How the Indians received their stipulated provisions, clothing, etc., may be illustrated by one example. It was in the year 1865. A large number of barrels of flour and meat were to be sent from Henderson, Sibley County, Minnesota, to Ft. Abercrombie. The contractors, in order to obtain the necessary conveyances at the lowest possible figure, deferred the delivery of these provisions so long that the whole train was snowed in over a hundred miles from the fort. The barrels were simply put on the open prairie and the teamsters came back. When the poor, half-starved Sioux were informed of this some time after, they started out to get the provisions, but instead of good flour they found bran and shorts, and flour made from spoiled wheat, which could not be used for bread; and yet the contractors received nearly fifteen dollars a barrel for the lot.

## 5. Schemes of the Traders

The principal agent divided the money allotted to the Indians among sub-officers and traders, who at the time of payment, received enormous sums of money for pretended services rendered and goods sold to the Indians. Contractors whose business it was to procure whatever was needed at the agency, such as provisions, horses, cattle, farming implements, etc., all charged enormously for their services. The Indians were to be supplied with good horses and cattle, but they received the worst and poorest, for which they had to pay five times the ordinary value. Not knowing the real value of such articles the Indian was constantly swindled. A valuable buffalo hide was frequently given for a pound of sugar. Many paid from three to five dollars for a single drink of whisky. A certain quantity of fuel was to be delivered to them annually. This was, despite their protests, cut from their own lands, after which they had to pay half price for it. A large mill was built of funds belonging to the Indians, and still they had to pay a high price for what milling products they bought there. House after house was erected for the Indians solely to give some contractor a chance to do the work. Many Indians had fine large brick residences erected but lived in tepees, and the agents knew they preferred the wild way of living, but build the structures to give men work who spent the money received at the traders' stores--a real graft game. One very interesting feature was how they were taught the different arts and sciences. Some employees were continually building fences only to be used as fuel by the Indians. They would plow and sow at all seasons of the year simply to show the Indian how it was done. One Randall, employed as a teacher, used to drive his pupils away from the school with a whip, but drew his salary amounting to several thousand dollars regularly.

## 6. The Indians' Protest

Every question, it is said has two sides, and before passing on to a description of the massacre of 1862, let the reader hear what was contended by old Chief Red Iron, as early as 1852--ten years before this outbreak. It was in December, 1852, that the chief of the Sisseton, Ma-zas-ha (Red Iron), was, on account of his bad behavior, to be deprived of his dignity as chief by Ramsey, the superintendent of Indian affairs.

Red Iron was the real type of an Indian chief, some six feet high, strongly built, had a finely shaped head, a prominent nose and piercing eyes. He was clad in the costume of a Dakota chief; about forty years old, shrewd, proud and determined, and answered boldly and promptly the questions and objections raised by Ramsey. As an orator he had much talent. When Ramsey insisted upon getting his signature for the purpose of retaining a considerable sum of money from funds belonging to the Indians in order to pay some old debts due the traders, Red Iron, raising himself to his full height, pressing his hand firmly upon his scalping knife, with a firm determined look at the agent, said:

"We want our pay, and we will sign no paper except a receipt for the money. The snow covers the ground, and we are still waiting for our money. We are very poor; you have plenty. Your fires burn well; your tents are well closed against the cold. We have nothing to eat. We wait a long time for our money. Many of our people are sick from hunger. We will have to die, because you do not pay us. We may die, and if so we will leave our bones unburied, so that our Great Father may see how his Dakota children died. We have sold our hunting grounds and no less the graves of our fathers. We also sold our own graves. We do not know where we shall bury our dead, and you will not pay the money for that land."

After this well-delivered speech was made he was taken a prisoner. The air began to tremble before the hideous yells of the Dakota warriors, and armed Indians hurried from all sides to a place upon which the bones of dead warriors were strewn about. Lean Bear, a favorite among the warriors of Red Iron's band, a determined and powerful Indian, dropped his blanket and grasped the scalping knife with his right hand and recounted all the great deeds of their imprisoned chief, whereupon they cried, "Ho! ho!" After that he said to them:

"Dakotas! The great men are among us; they hold Ma-zas-ha imprisoned like a wolf; they want to kill him because he prevents the white men to cheat us of our land and the money which the Great Father has sent us."

He was interrupted by a thundering "Ho! ho!" but continued:

"Dakotas! Shall we starve in the snow like buffaloes? Shall we permit our blood to freeze like the waters of a brook, or shall we paint the snow with the blood of white warriors?"

"Ho! ho!" answered the savages, he continued, "The blood of your fathers cries to you from their graves; their spirits embrace us and make us strong. I am glad of it. Even this very night shall the blood of the pale-faces flow like water in a shower, and Me-zas-ha shall fight with his people. Dakotas! As soon as the moon hides behind the hills prepare yourselves, and I will lead you against the long knives (bayonets and swords) of the white men who have come to swindle us, to rob us of our land, and to imprison us, because we do not assist them to rob our wives and children. Dakotas! Be without fear; we have more warriors than the whites. Be ready! When the moon sinks I will lead you to their tents." and the warcry resounded in the whole assembly.

"Dakotas!"

## 7. Organization of Young Warriors

Time went on and by December, 1861, the Indians, some fifteen hundred of them had to be cared for in order to keep them from starvation. Crops had been poor several years, bugs had ruined the crops only the summer before. A fearful snow storm came during the month of February, 1862, and this frustrated their hopes of soon being able to supply themselves with game. Under these circumstances they anxiously waited for the payday of 1862. They knew all about the great Civil War which was then in progress, and this increased their fears that the government might not be able to pay them. They also desired to see the North whipped, so that they might be enabled to complete the work. There are those who think that some who were in sympathy with the South did all they could to induce the Indians into mischief. Misled by unfavorable reports the Indians imagined that they had to fight only with old men, women and children, and that they had reason to fear that they never would receive any more money.

The different tribes went to the agency early to demand their pay. The agents told them they would receive their money, but did not know when, which caused great dissatisfaction among the Indians. In the course of time from five to six thousand were gathered there. All were full of fear and mistrust lest they might not receive their money. Their want was so great that many died of hunger, others lived on roots and raw corn. Reports were circulated by some of the whites that the government was becoming weaker day by day, and messengers began to go from one tribe to another planning the possibility and success of a revolt. The older and more intelligent among them were opposed to it; but the hot-headed, and especially the younger warriors, formed themselves into a secret society called "Soldiers' Lodge."

This secret society, established early in July, had for its object to oppose the traders and to prevent them from getting their money, and in case of necessity to defend their rights by force. The chiefs, although informed of this organization, did not dare oppose it. They well understood the dangers connected with it, since these young warriors numbered from five to six thousand; and the chiefs were even suspected of being in league with the officers of the government for suppressing and swindling their people. The traders soon learned about the Soldiers' Lodge and its object, and when the Indians wanted to buy something from them on credit, they were told to go to the Soldiers' Lodge. The Indians, compelled to ask for credit on account of their extreme need, would answer the traders: "If we could, like our women, give ourselves up to you, we could get all the credit we ask for; but since we are men we cannot."

## 8. First Act of Violence

And thus did bitterness increase during 1862. Those who were suspected of informing the traders and others of the doings of the society were severely persecuted, and some of them killed. Their first act of violence was committed on August 4, 1862. The time for payment was up in July. The want among the assembled tribes was alarmingly on the increase. Some of them had already devoured their own ponies and dogs. Six children had died of starvation within three days. Agent Galbraith traveled from one agency to another in order to pacify them; and sometimes distributed provisions, tobacco, powder and lead. But that was not sufficient to quiet the uneasiness caused by the delay of their pay. Early in the morning of the 4th of August, some five hundred and fifty young warriors, mostly members of Soldiers' Lodge, forced an entrance to the warehouse, tore down the American flag and took over one hundred and fifty sacks of flour before any resistance was offered, which could have been done, since there were one hundred well-armed soldiers with two heavy cannons nearby. The soldiers entered the warehouse and took possession of it whilst the Indians stood around with loaded rifles. But when the agent promised to furnish them with pork, rice, and flour the following day, they did not attempt any further disturbance.

The fact that not one of the warriors was punished for this serious breach of the peace made them bold and daring; and the more so when they saw the able men among the whites leave for the South at their country's call on the 13th, 14th and 15th of August. On the 18th of August, at eight o'clock a.m., they left New Ulm under Lieutenant Culver and Sergeant McGrew, as "Keyville Rangers," and on the same day the Indians broke out.

The time was now at hand which was to give the two Germans who had been murdered some time before numerous companions. A man named Brand had been put to death on the banks of the Little Cottonwood, six miles south of New Ulm, in the spring of 1857, and body was found in the brush near some Indian tepees. John B. Schmitz wanted to settle on the reservation ten miles west of New Ulm, but on the 27th of April, 1860, while digging a cellar, he was treacherously shot and killed.

The murderer, a Sioux, was imprisoned at New Ulm. During the trial in the court-room a heavy chain was attached to his feet, and he was well guarded. At a necessary call he desired to leave the room. Constable Charles Seeler obtained the assistance of his deputy, Doctor Blecken, a renowned physician who was at one time a Lutheran minister, but later a preacher at a free church; he was also one of the founders of New Ulm. To guard against any possible accident, a third deputy was called into service. But man proposed, and, in this instance, the Indian disposed. So soon as he was in the open air he managed to shake off his fetters, and with the swiftness of a deer the stalwart form of the Indian disappeared from before their astonished gaze. The three officers of the law, on account of the sudden and unexpected disappearance of their prisoner, were so stunned that they did not as much as remember their revolvers, which were left untouched in the official pockets. It was just at dusk and the Indian did not return. The trial was over. Such murders and the escape of the guilty ones caused much alarm in the country.

About the middle of August, 1862, Mail-carrier Miles was met by the Indians some two miles south of the Lower Agency and led out of his way across the prairie, because they were holding a secret meeting in a ravine on the bank of the river, where he would have observed them. A few days previous to this Miles noticed some newly-cut signs on the trees, apparently of great importance. About the same time friendly Indians warned the settlers of the approaching dangers saying: "Pakat-shif" (go away) and "Nip-po" (to kill). They also made signs with their hands which the whites did not want to understand or believe. A week or so before the outbreak, a number of gaudily dressed and decorated Indians held in the town of New Ulm those wild dances, which are always forebodings of evil. Their tomahawks and scalping knives were sharpened. The cause of the outbreak was evidently the neglect of a prompt fulfillment of duty on the part of the government officials, the extreme need of the Indians and delay of their annual pay. They were to receive their money in gold coin. The government sent the money promptly to St. Paul where it remained for a long time; but the officials in whose hands it had been placed, exchanged it for paper money at a great premium, in opposition to the loud protests of the officials at the Sioux money for distribution among the Indians they sent currency instead of coin, as was stipulated. The Indians not being accustomed to handle paper money, became greatly enraged so that the agents finally concluded to exchange it for gold. This, of course, caused a great loss, the premium being then very high. But they were little concerned about this, for they intended to make the Indians pay the discount. They soon found out, however, that they had been calculating without consulting the party most deeply interested in the transaction.

The anger of the Indians increased. They did not wait till the agent at St. Paul could make the necessary exchange (which required considerable time), but rose up everywhere and gave free scope to their sorely pent-up feelings of revenge. A settlement as sudden as it was violent, not in gold but in blood, was to balance the unjust accounts which had hitherto been kept between a civilized and a savage people. Suddenly and violently did the sword of vengeance fall upon the heads of those who would not believe that such could happen, even in the face of fire and sword. A proud trader named Myrick was much hated among the Indians, and they appeared in front of his store and said: "You have told us you would not give us anything on credit, though we were compelled to eat hay and verdure, or starve, during the winter. Now, then, be careful not to take water or wood from our reservation."

Myrick answered: "All right; but if you are cold, and want to warm yourselves at my stove, I will put you out of my house."

They had told the same to other traders and had received about the same answer. This was just before the outbreak.

## 9. Pillaging Leads to Murder

The more friendly chiefs were no longer able to prevent the young warriors, especially the members of the Soldiers' Lodge, from committing acts of violence. August 17 some twenty Indians went from the Lower Agency to Forest City, on a deer hunt. The chief, Wah-pe-yah-we-tah, separated himself with four Indians from the others. They originally belonged to the Upper Agency, but were connected with the Shakopees band and had a hard name. About six miles out of Acton, and thirty miles from the agency, one of the Indians found a hen's next, with eggs, in the field. He took one and advised others to take the rest. But one of the four said: "They are the eggs of a tame bird and they belong to a white man. You must not touch them."

"Nonsense," said the other, "they are not worth anything. We are hungry and we are justified in taking them."

"No," responded the latter, "they do not belong to us. It is wrong to take them; we will get into trouble with the paleface."

"Oh," said the former, "you are very virtuous. You Rice Creek Indians talk much against the whites, but you dare not take a few miserable eggs. I am not afraid of you miserable fools!"

"You must not talk about the paleface," said the other, "because he is not present. Vilify me, for I am here and am not afraid of your violent talk."

"To the devil with you and your eggs!" was the reply more vigorous than elegant; and down came the eggs.

"That is a very brave deed," said his companion, mockingly, "to destroy a few hen's eggs. You are a coward!"

The quarrel became more earnest and more bitter as they went on. All at once they spied a heifer, and the one who had broken the eggs cried out: "You say I am a coward. I am so courageous and fear the palefaces so little that I will kill one of their heifers. Look here!"

He leveled his rifle and shot the heifer.

"You call that bravery?" said the other. "I call it a cowardly act. You destroy eggs and kill an ox. You are a woman. I am a brave man and know what bravery is. I was in the war with the Chippewas and have taken scalps."

And thus they quarreled for a while longer till it nearly came to a fight, when the others stepped in and said:

"Since we cannot agree, we will part and take different roads. You will find out whether we are cowardly or brave. We will kill a paleface." And they separated. Soon after that they heard shots, and believing that those who had separated from them had killed some of the settlers, they thought they would do the same, so as not to appear to be cowards before the others. They, however, disagreed again. They passed a vacant house, but when they came to the next, the home of R. Jones, they went in. They soon began to quarrel with him about some eatables and a gun. Jones drove them away, and they entered another house which was the home of Howard Baker, Jones's son-in-law. There were two strangers with Baker (Mr. Webster and his wife), who had just arrived from Wisconsin with the intention of settling in that neighborhood.

The Indians asked for water and tobacco, which were given them. They were very quiet until Jones and his wife, who came to pay their daughter-in-law a visit, arrived. The quarrel between Jones and one of the Indians was renewed. Mrs. Baker asked her mother if she had given the Indians any whisky, to which she replied: "No, we have no whisky for such black devils as these."

The Indians seemed to have understood the answer, judging from their sudden excitement. Mrs. Webster requested Mrs. Jones to drop the matter. The Indians, however, were now ready for their deadly work. Jones was trying to sell Baker's gun to one of the Indians. The latter asked Jones to shoot and try the gun, probably with the intention of leaving an empty gun in his hands. Jones was willing to comply with this request, and remarked that he was not afraid to shoot with any of the cursed redskins. Webster did not want to do any shooting, although he had a gun. One of the Indians said that something was wrong with the hammer of his gun, and asked him to take his off and lend it to him. After the shooting was over the Indians reloaded their guns, but Jones and Baker neglected to reload theirs. Meanwhile one of the Indians had gone toward Forest City to find out whether there were any whites in the neighborhood. When he returned, the four Indians consulted together and acted as if they wanted to leave. Mrs. Jones and Mrs. Baker stood on the door-steps. Suddenly the Indians turned around, and one of them leveled his gun at Mrs. Baker. Her husband noticing this, threw himself at once between his wife and the Indian and received the deadly bullet. At the same moment Jones, Webster, and Mrs. Jones were shot. When Mrs. Baker, who held a child on her arm, saw her husband drop dead, she fainted and fell backward into the cellar, the door of which was open, and thus escaped death herself. Jones's children were also in the house, but were not noticed.

The Indians then returned to Jones's house and killed and scalped a girl. Her brother, who was lying on a bed saw it, but did not venture to stir. Mrs. Webster hid in a covered wagon and escaped. After the Indians had left Baker's house Mrs. Baker came out of the cellar, and, with the assistance of Mrs. Webster, who came out of the wagon placed pillows under the heads of the wounded. The situation of these poor women was deplorable. Their fright and despair, their loneliness and uncertainty of what the next moment might have in store for them, were intensified by the groans of the dying men. Jones, a strong and heavily built man, of extraordinary height, dark complexion, dark hair and beard, with a keen eye, was the very ideal of a cavalry officer. His strong constitution wrestled with death. In his agony he filled his mouth with dust, and, with his heels, dug deep hones in the ground, begging his wife to fly with the child. But she stayed with him until he died, and then fled into the woods.

During this fearful scene a white man passed by, who being requested by the women to help them, laughed and said: "They have only the nose-bleed, the Indians will soon come and finish them." The two women, on going toward the woods, entered the house of a Norwegian. They found only a boy at home, and they sent him at once to Ft. Ridgely with the terrible news. But the officers had so little faith in the boy's story that they waited a considerable time before sending a messenger to Forest City, where Captain Whitcomb had his recruits. Twelve mounted men were immediately dispatched to Acton, which they reached about dusk. Having placed a wagon-box over Jones's body to conceal it from the danger of mutilation, they did not disturb the others till the next morning.

The report of the terrible tragedy soon spread abroad and a large crowd gathered at the place to view the remains. Meanwhile, the Indians who had separated themselves from their criminal companions and were as yet ignorant of the crime, came within sight of the place. When they saw what happened there they fled with great speed across the swamp. The whites did not dare to follow them; but one bold man from Forest City pursued them and sent his bullets after them. One of the Indians jumped from his pony and shot back, but soon joined his companions again.

## 10. Tardy Action by the Government

These murders and the circumstances connected with them began to open the eyes of the whites as to their dangerous surroundings. Many of the Indians were now bolder and more defiant than ever. Fourteen of them had on the Sunday previous sharpened their knives and cleaned their rifles at a place five miles from Acton. It was therefore deemed absolutely necessary to send a messenger to the governor of the state, who soon reached St. Paul; but his story was not believed. The four Indians who had committed the crime in Acton went to Eckland's farm, near Elizabeth Lake and stole two horses, and with these drove as speedily as possible to the camp of Chief Shakopee, which they reached before dawn of the 18th of August. Sunday, August 17, was, therefore, the day which marked the beginning of those awful deeds of blood through which Minnesota was suddenly made so sadly famous.

There are those who think that when the four criminals related to their friends and relatives what they had done at Acton, the majority were of the opinion that the opportune time for a general butchery among palefaces had come; and in case this was not done they would have to bear the consequences of the crime already committed, but the fact that during the afternoon of this memorable Sunday a great council was held on Rice Creek, to which Indians had come a distance of forty miles, is sufficient evidence that this theory is false. The tragedy and this council took place about the same time, and the Indians who gathered there had no knowledge of the crime. It is also evident that this meeting had something to do with the outbreak; for at dusk—that is, soon after the meeting—the Indians appeared in war costume, their bodies painted and decorated with feathers, and half naked, mounted on their ponies, were galloping across the prairies from tribe to tribe to give the signal which was to be so fearful in its results for the poor settlers who had ventured to establish a home near the hunting grounds of the revengeful Indians.

The outbreak was well planned throughout. The savages had become so bold about that time that the officers and soldiers who went from New Ulm to Ft. Ridgely on the 17th of August remarked that something must be going on, and that it would be well to get ready for them.

A "draft" was about this time being ordered all over the United States to replace the soldiers who had died on Southern battle-fields. The young settlement at New Ulm and vicinity sent her best men for the maintenance of the Union, never suspecting that a cruel and more formidable enemy that the rebel of the South was at her very doors. On Monday, August 28, 1862, a number of citizens of New Ulm went toward the Lower Agency to a hall, about six miles from New Ulm, to be drafted.

The place belonged to A. Henle. They were accompanied by a band of music. Henle's place was located south of the Minnesota on the edge of the prairie and hard by the road which runs along the edge of the forest. When the company from New Ulm had nearly reached Henle's house the joyful strains of music were suddenly changed into profound sorrow and wailing. A few hundred steps from the place is a ravine which carried the waters of the prairie through the forest to the Minnesota River. The entrance to the ravine is thickly covered with timbers close up to the bridge which spans it. When the teams approached this bridge several shots were fired from the ravine by Indians who had been lying in wait for them. Three of the company fell dead—John Schneider, Julius Fenske and A. Diederich. A man named Haupt lost one of his eyes, and another named Steinle was mortally wounded and died near Belleplaine on his way to St. Paul.

The first two teams were captured by the Indians. Those who could, fled across the prairie. The other teams were quickly turned and driven in all haste back to New Ulm. This took place between eleven and twelve o'clock a.m. It was impossible for them to offer resistance, not one of them being armed. While the shooting was going on, those in the rear of the train were in the act of picking up Joseph Messner, who but a few minutes before had been wounded by the Indians and had not been noticed by the others at the time. Besides other fatal wounds inflicted on him, they had cut off one of his arms and one of his ears. He was brought back to town, but he died after suffering great agony for twenty-four hours.

Just then three well-armed men arrived from Garden City. They had heard rumors there about a massacre, but they believed them to have been originated by a few drunken men. When they were shown the mutilated body of Joseph Messner they began to think differently.

## 11. Beginning of the Massacre

The beginning of the massacre was made at the home of Mr. Massapust, Bohemian immigrants. Their house was located on the road between New Ulm and the Lower Agency, and was first reached by the Indians who came from there. Like blood-thirsty tigers they soon covered the whole settlement, so the attack on the different families happened at almost the same time, thus one neighbor could not warn another. At Massapust's place father, mother and two daughters were massacred in a most cruel manner, the two latter having suffered the most horrible and shameful outrages at the hands of the Indian warriors. Only one boy, eight years old, fled and was saved. According to reports he was murdered by the Sioux several years later, having killed a number of Indians, which he vowed to do as an act of revenge for the death of his family. Massapust's house was located near the Henle place, eight miles out of New Ulm.

## 12. Other Bloody Deeds

Caroline (Zicher) Stocker, wife of Joseph Stocker, from Erbach, Wuerttemberg, was lying sick when the Indians reached her house. She had always been kind to them, and properly thought that they might spare her. But, no; she was unmercifully shot in her bed, and her body burnt with the house. Her husband fled with the ten-year-old Cecilia Ochs into the celler. The Indians fastened the door and set the house on fire. In their despair the two prisoners opened with a shingle a place under the sill of the burning building and escaped into the woods without being noticed by the savages.

Florian Hartman and one Rohner, a Swiss, who was working for him, were shot in the field on the same day. The mother of Carl Pelzl, the parents of Louis Thilling and one Haag, were also killed in the same neighborhood. Pelzl's father was seriously wounded and died later. All these families lived in the same district, six to eight miles northwest from New Ulm. Only a few from this settlement made their escape. Among those were Athanasius Henle, who had received timely warning and fled with his wife and children on horseback through the woods and across the Minnesota River. The families of Casimer and Ochs, and Conrad Zeller, also escaped.

The panic among the settlers, their helpless condition, fright, and despair cannot be described. The prairie was covered with men on horseback, carrying the terrible news from house to house, and cries of fear and woe were rending the air. The most necessary articles of furniture that could be easily carried were picked up, and the dear home was deserted, and everybody hurried to the town of New Ulm, their eyes continually wandering over the prairies in quest of the dreadful enemy. Some did not even take time to get their teams or anything else in order. Others, intent only upon saving their lives, fled as soon as they heard the rifle shots and saw columns of fire.

Toward the evening of August 18, a perfect stream of fugitives began to pour into New Ulm. The excitement was greatly increased at the sight of the mutilated bodies that were brought into town from Milford (Henle's settlement). There could be no longer any doubt the approaching danger. The cry: "Fly, for the Indians have gone on the war-path!" now had a terrible meaning to the minds of the settlers. New Ulm, Ft. Ridgely, and further down, Mankato and St. Peter were the desired places of refuge for the settlers. Since Ft. Ridgely was soon surrounded by the Indians, and Mankato and St. Peter were too distant (these places lie from twenty-eight to thirty miles east), New Ulm had to shelter most of the fugitives.

At two o'clock in the afternoon of August 18, Jacob Nix reached Pfaender's place on the road from Ft. Ridgely to New Ulm, where he notified the wife and children of the outbreak. Pfaender was at that time amid the scenes of war in the South. They would not believe the report until Nix began to put the children and some of the bedding into his wagon, assuring the poor woman that the Indians might be upon them at any moment. Having a good team of horses he soon reached town with his charge. Approaching New Ulm, where the outbreak had been reported a few hours before, he mistook one of the out-lying pickets for an Indian, and in his excitement was about to open fire on him when he discovered that it was a friend of his named Rudolph.

## 13. Captain Nix in Command

When he arrived in town he found the citizens organizing a volunteer company, for which purpose one Czeigowitz, formerly an Austrian soldier, placed fifty men in line in front of the Dakota House. As soon as Nix made his appearance he was unanimously elected commander of the company. He was known as an old soldier who had fought in Algiers and had been captain of a company during a revolution in that country. He was born or reared at that famous village every schoolboy has read of Bingen-on-the-Rhine. He was later a captain under General Sulley in the Indian War of the Northwest. Sheriff Roos administrated the formal oath to Captain Nix and he then took command. A few days later, however, Judge Charles E. Flandrau was sent by the governor and took command of the forces. But Sheriff Roos believed the murders to have been committed by a few drunken Indians; consequently it would be his duty as sheriff to imprison the offenders. Accompanied by twenty-five men he immediately started out toward the scene of the massacre, six miles from town. When they saw the dead bodies covered with blood and terribly mutilated, and being themselves attacked by some of the Indians from a distance, they changed their minds and believed it to be a real outbreak. Then they began to look for an gather the dead and wounded, and carried them to New Ulm. So far, the sheriff's erroneous idea about the matter served a good purpose. When the wagons carrying the wounded and the dead reached New Ulm, the excitement among the people also reached its climax. Considering the state of affairs as they then stood, it could easily be seen that the worst was yet to come. Many wanted to leave town immediately, others thought differently. These did not want to give up their homes so easily, and it was to be expected that many more people from the country would seek refuge in town. Their means for defending the town against an attack were, however, very poor. Still they could more easily defend themselves behind barricades in town than on the open prairie; and if they would try to go St. Peter or Mankato, a distance of about thirty miles, they would most likely be attacked by the Indians on the way.

It was now Monday evening, and strict orders were given to provide all possible means of defense. Fugitives were captured and brought back. They began to throw up a breast-work, and sent Henry Behnke and Schwerdtfeger as couriers to St. Peter and Mankato, asking for immediate assistance. These preparations infused courage and hope into the fearfully-excited minds of the people, although they did not have more than fifty guns for defense. Many of these were old, rusty and useless articles, such as peaceful citizens keep in their homes more for ornament than for use. There were only twelve rifles, and the fate of two thousand people was depending upon them. In their extreme need they looked for other means of defense. Anything that might serve to frighten the enemy was considered good for the purpose. Here could be seen several companies armed with axes, scythes and pitchforks.

On account of the residences in New Ulm being far apart, except those on Minnesota Street, which was then the main street of the city, they had to limit their fortifications to about four blocks. There were only three brick blocks in New Ulm at that date. They belonged to Foster, Flick and Erd, and were chosen as places of refuge for the women and children, and included in the fortified section of the place. Weddendorf also had a brick house; but it was too far out to serve any good purpose. The work of building fortifications went on during the whole night, from the 18th to the 19th of August. Old wagons, barrels, logs, fuel, etc., were engaged in casting bullets. Fires were kept up, the numerous pickets that had been sent out, the coming in of fugitives, all telling different but equally sad stories, left an impression on the peaceful settlers that time cannot blot from their memories.

## 14. Indians Besiege the Town

On Tuesday morning, August 19, the people began to breathe easier. A night of anxiety and care, during which they expected a cruel and unmerciful enemy to fall upon them at any moment, had now passed away. At the break of day H. Brockman, a surveyor, placed himself on the flat roof of Erd's residence, and by means of a telescope examined the country around New Ulm. About eleven o'clock families arriving from the Cottonwood settlement reported that the Indians were beginning to cut the fugitives off from New Ulm. In order to assist these, one Spenner was sent out with twelve men armed with rifles; and fourteen others were sent out under one Prunk, armed with double barreled shot guns. The later returned with a large number of fugitives from the Cottonwood settlement. The first party that went out did not return; they had gone on too far. Their absence caused great uneasiness, because they had taken with them the only good arms that New Ulm had.

Meanwhile Mr. Swift, who later became governor of the state of Minnesota, came to town from St. Paul, with five others, on business. According to the custom of those days they were well armed and provided with excellent rifles. No sooner had they learned of the state of affairs than they wanted to turn back; but they were finally persuaded by Captain Nix to remain.

About three o'clock p.m., Brockman gave information that in the direction of the agency, near Hoffman's farm, Indians could be seen riding out on the open prairie. Excitement and terrible fear now reigned supreme once more. Indians came from a northwesterly direction toward New Ulm, from the side where the cemeteries are now located. They kept close together as they came in on their ponies; but when within a short distance from town they separated, and in a few minutes the place was surrounded. The scene was well calculated to strike terror into the hearts of the people. The Indians were almost entirely naked, covered only with their hideous war-paint. Every movement indicated their savage thirst for blood. They filled the air with barbarous yells, and boldly challenged the white man, the representative of culture and civilization, to a fight. What a sight for a poor helpless people to behold! Woe to the white man who fell into the hands of so terrible a foe!

Captain Nix immediately ordered his men to the barricades. At first he could gather only twenty men, and but six of these had the courage to fall in line. The Indians had approached, and, throwing themselves upon the ground, commenced firing, which made sad havoc among the defenders. Against their magnificent rifles the arms of the settlers were a mere nothing. Captain Nix received a bullet in the right hand which shattered one of his fingers. The fourteen-year-old daughter of one Pauly, who, out of curiosity, had left Erd's residence to see the beginning of the fight, was hit by this same bullet, which entered her forehead and killed her instantly.

Spenner's detachment very fortunately returned at the beginning of the fight. They brought with them many fugitives, and, united together, they forced their way into town. The fight lasted about two hours. The Indians numbered several hundred. But these seemed to have been only the advance guard of the army, who boldly attempted to take and plunder the town before the others could arrive. Three houses were set on fire during the attack, of which Bellm's residence was the first. A heavy rain was pouring down, and this had a great deal to do with saving the town. Frederick Pouser received a wound on his neck from the effects of which he was a constant sufferer up to the time of his death, May 1876. He left a very large family.

As soon as the fight was over and the Indians had retreated, the first reinforcements arrived from St. Peter, consisting of twenty-five horsemen under the command of Sheriff Boardmann. The proposal of Captain Nix that these twenty-five men should pursue the Indians was not accepted.

The same day several citizens met with a very sad death. Under various pretexts they left New Ulm in the morning. Over a dozen armed men, among whom were Carroll, Tuttle, Thomas, Loomis brothers, Ives, Kirby, Coon, Lemmon, Lamb and Jinton, left New Ulm. Neither the advice of their friends nor the fact that the defense of the town was thereby considerably weakened could prevent them from leaving. Moreover, they believed they were well able to defend themselves against a considerable number of Indians. Their homes were west of New Ulm, near Iberia on the Cottonwood and they wanted to go there to save their friends and the families they had left behind. Some of them had come to New Ulm on business, not being aware of the outbreak. Partly out of curiosity, and partly with the intention of warning settlers, they entered several houses on the way. Everywhere they went they found bodies of the dead. Here and there they discovered children, many of whom were wounded; and these they took with them. When they reached their homes they found neither Indians nor whites. On their way back to New Ulm they separated, some going south and others north of the Cottonwood, toward town, in order to discover and save some of the settlers who were said to have been dispersed over the prairie by the Indians. They had agreed to unite again at Tuttle's place and return to town together. When the first party, who had been searching on the north side of the Cottonwood, reached Tuttle's place, they found that the other party had already left for town. A man coming from New Ulm told them that he had met the others on the way.

## 15. A Fatal Ambush

When the second party, among whom were Carroll, Loomis, Lamb, Ryan (who had in the meantime joined them), Hinton and a Norwegian, noticed a fire in the neighborhood of New Ulm, stretching for about a mile from north to south, Hinton rode far enough in advance of the others to see the town from a hill. Returning to his companions he said that the town had just been attacked by the Indians, and proposed to take another road and fly to Mankato. This advice was rejected by the majority who reproached him for cowardice. They took a good view of the town and its surroundings, and could see only a few Indians. From there a good road leads to New Ulm; first across a swamp, then over a piece of slowly rising prairie, on the east side of which it leads directly to the town. They could have reached there in five minutes if the road had been clear. Carroll proposed that they force their way, and Hinton took the lead. When they came to the foot of the hill, near the swamp, they noticed two Indians who had been hiding behind a big rock leveling their rifles at the first horseman. Hinton drew his revolver and drove them back. But when they reached the other side of the swamp, those Indians who were hiding in the grass opened fire on them. Carroll, Almond, Loomis, Lamb, Ryan and the Norwegian fell dead at the first volley; the other two escaped into town. The second half of the expedition came about half an hour later and approached the place where so many of their companions had lost their lives. Not seeing Indians anywhere, they had no idea that at the end of the swamp they would run into a terrible trap. But no sooner had they left the east end of the swamp and were within a short distance of town, than suddenly more than a hundred blood-thirsty savages rose up from the tall grass and poured into them a shower of bullets. Six men and five horses fell dead. Thomas escaped. His horse was shot under him, but throwing away his gun he ran and reached town safely. An Indian sent two shots after him, but the bullets only struck the ground and covered him with dust. He was the only one of the second portion of that expedition who brought the news of the terrible fate of his companions to New Ulm. Two of the first party escaped by jumping on the front part of a wagon. The horses had become frightened and ran furiously toward town. Near the present side of the Lutheran church one of the men was shot and fell from the wagon, where he lay all night. He was mortally wounded and died the next morning; the other clung to the pole and reached town unharmed.

The place near the swamp gave evidence of the fight. Pieces of broken rifles were lying around on the trampled ground, and everywhere were traces of the fearful struggles of the dying men. A large stone marks the place to this day. On the body of one of them, who was not discovered till a few weeks later, a pocketbook with $800 was found. He had probably been seriously wounded, and, creeping away into a thicket to conceal himself, he died there. Thus was the fool-hardiness of these men, who were so eager to show their courage, terribly punished.

The loss of so many strong and courageous citizens and the gain for the Indians of so many rifles were not calculated to ease the minds of the terrified people. The heavy rain storm that came toward evening was a great blessing, for the Indians were thereby prevented from keeping up the siege and the danger of fire was lessened. The great uneasiness which overcame all when night approached was succeeded by much joy, for about midnight the watchmen announced the arrival of a large troop of horsemen. At first some were afraid they might be reinforcements for the hostiles. But the joyful tidings were soon announced that they were the men who, under command of the noble Charles E. Flandrau, had come from St. Peter and LeSueur to risk their lives in the defense of their neighbors. Their arrival brought joy to every heart. The town now had one hundred and fifty able defenders, well armed. This was about midnight of Tuesday and Wednesday. There were now some 1,500 persons in the fortified quarters of the town. Every available place was occupied. Flandrau was chosen commander-in-chief. He brought with him four physicians, Doctors Ayers and Mayo from LeSueur, and Doctors McMahon and Daniels from St. Peter. These relieved the overburdened Doctor Weschcke, who had been up to that time the only physician in New Ulm.

On Wednesday steps were taken to provide the necessary supplies. The barricades were improved and everything was done to be able to successfully resist the attack which was momentarily expected. During the day fifty volunteers arrived from Mankato under Captain Bierbauer, and an equal number from LeSueur. Nothing more could be seen of the Indians in the vicinity of New Ulm during those painful hours. Those who had been killed near town the day previous were picked up and buried and the wounded brought in and nursed.

## 16. Siege of New Ulm Continued

During those days, which proved to be a real blessing for New Ulm, the booming of cannon could be heard from Ft. Ridgely, and this encouraged the citizens to increase their fortifications. Even women and children gave a hand, for they were engaged in preparing bandages and casting bullets. They served a good purpose. On the morning of August 23, smoke clouds were seen rising everywhere. The surrounding farmhouses had been set on fire by the Indians. The redskins came flocking towards town on all sides. Among them was a very conspicuous chief riding a white pony. It was probably Little Crow himself. The first advance of the half-naked and gaudily-painted savages who, amidst a howling more like that of demons than of human beings, came storming on and drove the pickets in from their two widely scattered fortifications. Unfortunately, seventy-five men had just been sent across the river into Nicollet County to the Lafayette settlement, a few miles from New Ulm, because early in the day columns of smoke had been seen rising there. Lieutenant W. Huey tried in vain to get back to New Ulm. A number of Indians cut off their retreat. On his return, or rather his flight, he met Captain St. Julien Cox, on his way from St. Peter to New Ulm. But the Indians were strong enough to prevent both companies from entering New Ulm, and so they united on the open prairie for their common defense. Seventeen of them, however, forced their way through the hostile ranks, and, taking possession of the windmill fought till towards evening against a band of Indians who had taken possession of a hall nearby. After nightfall they set fire to the windmill and entered the barricades near the Dakota House.

Several other buildings, among them two mills, which were of little use to the Indians during the siege, were burned by them. Commander Flandrau desired to save what could be saved. Captain Nix had advised the destruction of the several residences outside the fortified quarters, but Flandrau would not consent to it. The Indians then made use of these residences with great advantage to themselves, keeping up a destructive fire on Minnesota Street. Flandrau then resolved that they had to be taken if New Ulm was to be saved. Captain Nix, with fifty men, mostly farmers, vigorously supported him, and received a bullet in the same arm from which he had lost a finger a few days before. After a stubborn resistance the Indians were driven out at about five o'clock in the afternoon, and the buildings, to save further danger, set on fire.

The besieged now began to burn down all the buildings outside the line which seemed to be in their way. A mania for the burning houses had taken so firm a hold, that, even inside the fortified quarters, Anton Zecher's residence was destroyed. Michelowski, a Pole, was so possessed by the fire-fiend that he had to be imprisoned, and Flandrau issued a proclamation to the effect that anyone caught in the act of setting fire to buildings would be shot. The Turner hall and the unfinished Catholic church, both main strongholds for the Indians, were fired.

There was now only one building standing outside the town, except the four blocks enclosed by the barricades. It was Weddendorf's residence, and was situated about one thousand yards north of the city limits. In it were stationed Zieher, Haeberle, the two Held brothers, Theobald, Hartneck, Bobleter (father of a subsequent postmaster), Kahlfeld, Hammer and nine others, in order to defend the town from that side. On account of inadequate means they did not succeed well. It being a newly-built brick house, the Indians wisely kept at a distance, and only a few were killed. The great number of warriors and their vigorous actions compelled these men to leave the place, and under cover of night cross the Minnesota and get into Nicollet County. Running toward Swan Lake they entered a swamp where they had to remain all night. J. Hartneck alone remained in the house. Anxiety and fear had so worked upon his mind that he became unconscious of danger. Toward morning he ran into town, receiving five shots, none of which proved fatal. Subsequently Hartneck died as a result of being injured by a mowing machine.

The besieged of New Ulm defended themselves like the valiant Greeks at the Pass of Thermopylae. They had the courage of lions, and met with better success than their Spartan prototypes. They were constantly prepared for any emergency. Most of the women and children were in the cellars under brick houses, and these were so filled that there was hardly any standing room left. With heroic courage and self-denial, they remained in their chosen prisons always ready for the worst. The most dreadful suspense these women suffered was the fear of the victorious war cry of the red demons, which was worse than death to them.

## 17. Narrow Escape of Women and Children

In Erd's cellar, in which the greater number of women and children were huddled together, there was a barrel of powder in charge of the widow of the late John Schmitz. It was held in readiness to blow up the building as soon as the Indians entered victorious. This fact was a menace to the whole town. Some cowardly wretches, it is said, had entered the cellar several times crying out that the town was taken. But womanly prudence and a mistrust, which would have been wrong at any other time, prevented a terrible catastrophe. Many may consider the intention which prompted these preparations not justified, and altogether wrong. But when the terrible fate which awaited the women and children, is taken into consideration, it is not fair to condemn their action.

During the whole night from Saturday to Sunday the fight was going on. It was truly a night of terror, because the citizens had to fight against an enemy who knew not mercy for either women or children, and who, thirsting for blood, was dreadfully in earnest to avenge his wrongs upon the innocent as well as the guilty. The crack of rifles, the whizzing of bullets, the wild yells of the Indians, the moans of the wounded and dying, the cries of frightened children, the surrounding darkness; these things were not calculated to fill the minds of the people with courage and hope. They rather filled the minds of the most courageous with fear. And then came the thought that the Indians might have taken possession of Ft. Ridgely, and, in possession of its instruments of death, nothing would be left of New Ulm. But the men stood bravely and firm at the barricades. They were all heroes, and, valiantly exposing their breasts to the deadly bullets of the enemy, they quietly sent like angels of death, their own dreadful summons to their terrible foe. There was, however, no lack of misunderstandings. Captain Dodd and others lost their lives in a very careless manner by making a sortie from the barricades in order to drive the Indians back. They were, of course, unmercifully butchered only a few steps from the barricades. The Indians made a fortunate mistake of too heavily charging their rifles, and, on this account, often shot above the mark.

A baker named Castor wanted to carry bread to some hungry customers, and being obliged to expose himself to the fire of the hostiles, put on a buffalo robe so as to appear like an Indian. A white man took him for one of them and of course shot him.

An old man named Roepke was crazed by fear and left the fortifications, and his body was afterward found frightfully mutilated.

What a relief it must have been to those brave people when, at the break of day, the Indians began to disperse! The Lord's Day–it was Sunday, August 24–brought salvation and safety. How many of the Indians were killed cannot be estimated, since they took with them when at all possible the dead and wounded. But the quantity of blood discovered around the city gave evidence of a terrible loss to them.

New Ulm had only eight dead and sixty wounded. Many of the latter died on account of its being impossible to give them the necessary care. One hundred and forty-nine residences were destroyed. Between nine and ten o'clock, Captain Cox managed to get into town with seventy-five men. Soon after that all the Indians retreated and held a council, whereupon they left altogether. Their main camping ground was in the neighborhood of the present Catholic cemetery. It is said that their sudden retreat was partly caused by a piece of strategy. It is well known that nothing can terrify the Indians so much as artillery. An inventive genius placed a stovepipe upon a cart, and two anvils were used for making the necessary noise. The Indians were thereby made to believe that a cannon had arrived during the night.

Captain Cox had been charged by the Governor to command the people to leave the town as soon as possible. Some refused to leave, especially Captain Nix. They were of the opinion that, after they were now somewhat secure and had gone through so much, they ought not so easily give up their homes to their enemy. Their victories had thus far made them proud and courageous, and they did not think it necessary to fly from even so formidable an enemy. The majority, however, were in favor of leaving the city, and the minority willingly gave in, in consideration of the many women and children and wounded men. Moreover, it was almost impossible for the two thousand five hundred persons to find accommodations in the forty-nine houses that had remained intact. Provisions were wanting. The numerous dead animals that were lying in and around town exposed to the hot summer sun soon would have filled the air with a stench that would have made a stay impossible. Sunday afternoon, preparations were made for removing to Mankato, twenty-eight miles from New Ulm. Monday morning, August 25, a long caravan–some in wagons, others on horses, and others on foot–moved towards Mankato. There were in line one hundred and fifty wagons, of which fifty-six were carrying the sick and wounded. The deserted city presented a very melancholy aspect. On account of the scarcity of teams many articles of furniture which had been so anxiously protected by their owners had to be left behind. All manner of things were lying about in the deserted houses and in the streets. Of the hundreds of articles only the more important and valuable had been removed. Some tried to carry household utensils on their shoulders, but, finding it inconvenient if not impossible, dropped them. The road between New Ulm and Mankato was therefore covered with miscellaneous household furniture. Nearly everything to which they had become devotedly attached had to be left behind in order to save their lives. The extent of the loss and the seriousness of the situation increased their sorrow more and more; and many a scalding tear was shed as the stricken people looked back upon their lost treasures. But the saddest of all were those who numbered their kindred among the dead, and who were obliged to leave them unburied on hostile ground. These things were more painful and oppressive than wounds. There were lonesome hearts in that sad procession, anxious to know what had become of father or mother, husband or wife, sister or brother or child.

## 18. Order Restored

When they reached Mankato orders were received to bring the sick and the wounded as well as the women and children to St. Peter, twelve miles farther. The able-bodied men were retained to assist in defending the town, since the Winnebago Indians were reported to have gone on the warpath. This separation of families was a new source of anxiety and sorrow. On reaching St. Peter the wounded and the helpless received all possible care and attention at the hands of its noble-hearted citizens. A few days before many of the fugitives who had arrived there from West Newton could get nothing to eat, because the people of St. Peter did not believe the report of an outbreak. There were so many sick and wounded that the private residences could not accommodate them all; the Catholic church was therefore turned into a temporary hospital. Later on, many wounded and sick, and also the women and children, were removed down the Minnesota River to other towns—LeSueur, Henderson, Belleplaine, Shakopee, and even to St. Paul.

After a few days, many of the citizens of New Ulm returned, for they had learned that a regular militia regiment and a number of well-armed volunteers had gone out in pursuit of the Indians. The defense of the town had no regular militia, but was made up in a hurry of all kinds of people, including farmers, mechanics and laborers.

The sufferings which they had endured, the almost irreparable loss of property and the dread of a repetition of these same trials were the causes why a number of the people of New Ulm and its vicinity did not return to their homes. St. Paul, Cincinnati and Chicago received many of the fugitives of that time. Many thus obtained fine farms for a few dollars which were even then worth more than as many thousands.

It took quite a while, however, before immigration to New Ulm and its surroundings made any real progress, because the Indians continued for a long time after the outbreak to harass the settlers. It was hardly a year after that when Athanasius Henle was shot at by the Indians, on his way to town, in broad daylight. He escaped without injury. Not far from there a man named Bosche was shot dead the same day while working on what is now Pfaender's farm, just as his three sons were bringing him his dinner. But when, a few years later, the United States government indemnified the people for their losses as far as money could do it, a golden era opened for New Ulm and vicinity. Immigrants continued to come, and they brought with them wealth and prosperity.

# III. Personal Accounts

## 19. The Milford Massacre[11]

In the year 1854 a party of land-seekers and home-builders from Chicago, going westward, arrived at what is now the city of New Ulm, Minnesota, in October of the year, and crossed what is now the township of Milford, Brown county, then a complete wilderness. The party being satisfied that at last they had found good, fertile land with plenty of timber, looked for a suitable place for encampment for the winter, and finally built a log shanty near the Minnesota River, opposite the place of a certain Joseph La Framboise, a French-Canadian, who proved to be a friend indeed to the newcomers, in helping wherever he could to tide over the extremely cold and severe winter. In the middle of the winter their log shanty burned down and they considered themselves in luck to find a few abandoned Indian tepees (barkhuts) in which they lived the rest of the winter. I shall not try to describe the hardships and sufferings these people experienced during that time, as one must have had a similar experience to fully understand the situation. When at last spring came as a deliverer, they looked the country over for a suitable townsite, with a good attractive surrounding country for farming purposes, and finally decided upon the place where the beautiful city of New Ulm now stands. Those who preferred country life settled in the township immediately west of the townsite, in what is now the township of Milford. The land in question had in the treaty of Traverse Des Sious, been ceded to the United States by the Indians. The Indians of the Sioux or Dakota tribe were friendly to the whites and in no way molested them, although they continued to hunt on the land ceded by them to the government. Settlers began to come in considerable numbers, and in 1857 every quarter section open for settlement had been pre-empted; the western line of the same being about six and one-half miles west of the city limits of New Ulm, where the Indian reservation (land owned by the Indians) commenced. The Indians being our near neighbors, naturally visited us quite frequently, some out of curiosity, others for the purpose of begging—and in the art of begging the Indian is

---

11 Christopher Spelbrink, a resident of New Ulm, has written his recollections of the Indian troubles in Brown County—especially as to the "Milford Massacre," in which his family suffered, as well as his views concerning the general causes leading up to the awful Indian War of August, 1862.

hard to beat—but they never offered any serious molestations, or unfriendliness, until that terrible day, the 18th of August, 1862.

The first settlers (recalled by me), and those who came in the autumn of 1854, with untiring efforts to find a suitable place for a settlement, who braved the hardships and solitude of the wilderness, holding on till their efforts were crowned with success, are as follow: Ludwig Meyer, Sr., Joseph Dambach, Athanasius Henle, John Zettel, Franz Massapust, Peter Mack, Alois Palmer, Anton Henle, M. Wall, Vincent Brunner, Elizabeth Fink and Barbara Tuttle. Of all this little band, so far as I know, Peter Mack is the only survivor—all the rest have answered to the last call.

## 20. Cause of the Outbreak

The Indians in selling their lands for a price that was simply nominal, were promised by contract by the government, to receive their payments in gold, in twenty yearly installments at a certain time and at their agencies; the Lower Agency about eight miles east of what is now Redwood Falls, and the Upper Agency near the Yellow Medicine River. In both of these agencies were storekeepers or Indian traders, who had the exclusive Indian trade, and when payday came, the Indian who received his pay in cash was considered very fortunate; how this could happen I will try to explain; some of the Indians, perhaps the majority of them, could not, and especially when the buffalo hunt had been bad, make both ends meet, so to say, till the next payday, consequently they bought on credit, which was allowed them to some extent, the trader, of course, knowing how much money the Indian was entitled to, was very careful not to allow too much. When payday came, which was usually in June of each year, a large party of annuity Indians (Indians entitled to payment) assembled at the agency, waiting for the arrival of the paymaster.

The paymaster, his assistants and the Indian traders take their places at a table which is surrounded by a squad of soldiers, who have been ordered from Ft. Ridgely, for the purpose of keeping order and to prevent any disturbance. The Indians waiting for the call of their names; an Indian is called; he steps into the enclosure, the agent counts off the sum he is entitled to, and is about to receive it when the trader or storekeeper steps in, presenting to the agent a bill against the said Indian, and most of the money, perhaps all, is simply handed to the trader or storekeeper without any further question, and the Indian is dismissed to make room for another, and in a great many cases this procedure is repeated. Now, the trader cannot be accused of cheating the Indians, as they can neither read nor write, so all the advantage is on the side of the storekeeper or trader, and he certainly is not in business for his health. Then there is another line where the Indian is badly beaten, the fur trade. The most valuable furs are sold by the Indians, who are as a rule ignorant of the true value, for far less than one-half of the valuation, which is given them in the way of cheap goods. Add to this the very excessive profit the trader takes, and what is really left to the Indian is practically not worth mentioning. To this is added the illegal sale of bad whiskey by some unscrupulous whites or half-breeds, and as a rule the Indians are cleaned out of every cent in a very short time, as an Indian will pay almost any price for whisky by some unscrupulous whites or half-breeds, and as trade. When at last, he finds out how badly he has been beaten, his grudge against the whites increases and true to his nature, he is waiting patiently, for the time to get even, and it becomes his fixed opinion, that all whites are thieves and scoundrels, whose only aim is to beat the poor Indian and while this, of course, is exaggerated, in a good many cases is undoubtedly true. The Indian's nature is savage, brutal and cruel, and when in his opinion the time for revenge and retaliation has come, he makes no distinction between guilty and innocent. His savage nature is his only guide. In his lust and desire for blood he will surpass the tiger of the jungle; murder and torture are his enjoyment, and the proverbial imps of hell cannot outdo him in cruelty.

In the year 1861 the buffalo hunt had been very unsuccessful, and in consequence of which the Indians were in want of provisions, as dried buffalo meat is an important factor as a means of subsistence, so in the winter of 1861-62 there existed great want among the Indians, and in some cases, especially among the infants, actual starvation. The government at both agencies had caused some land to be plowed and planted to corn, potatoes, etc., for the benefit of the Indians, but that could not do away or diminish in any way the present dire need, and making the situation still worse, the news had spread amongst the Indians that they were to receive no pay that year, as the government needed the money for the war against the Southern rebellion. This, of course, was unfounded, but it aroused the savages, who organized into the so-called "Soldiers' Lodge," who appearing in considerable numbers, broke into the government warehouse, and in the presence of a company of soldiers, began carrying out such provisions as they wanted, flour, bacon, etc. Finally, the soldiers having taken possession of the warehouse, the Indians, after a quantity of flour, pork, etc., was divided among them, were persuaded to disperse and go to their homes and not come back until the next payday, which somewhat later than usual, would surely come. To this the Indians agreed and sullenly left.

About the latter part of July, the Indian agent or paymaster arrived at the Lower Agency, and the Indians were called together to receive their pay, when it developed that the agent instead of paying them in gold, as agreed, tried to pay them in currency. Here for the first time, the agent had reckoned without the host, for the Indians positively refused to accept the paper money. Here again, was an attempted swindle on a somewhat larger scale. In 1862 on account of the stringency in money (gold coin) caused by the Civil War then in progress, gold commanded a very high premium, nearly if not quite two times the value of paper money. The government, so it is claimed, sent the gold to the agent, who was accused of selling same for paper money and intending to give the Indians dollar for dollar and pocket the profit for his own personal use, but for once this scheme did not work out, so all the agent could do was to take his paper money and exchange it for gold. This, of course, could not be done in a hurry, but that did not matter. The Indians must wait. After the agent had left for the East to make his exchange, matters with the Indians went from bad to worse, as they had waited overtime and were in sore need of the money.

On Sunday, the 17th of August, the Indians held a great meeting, which of course was secret, but late in the day, mounted Indians (probably messengers) were seen to gallop in different directions over the prairie, and so the day closed.

## 21. Vengeance on the Traders

On the 18th of August, 1862, early in the morning, inhabitants of the Lower Agency were aroused by the sudden report of gunfire, and were very quickly aware of its meaning. Crack! Went the Indian gun and down went the trader, for the traders or storekeepers were the first upon whose heads fell the vengeance of the Indians. Few, if any, escaped. The superintendent of Indian affairs at the agency, August Wagner, saw the Indians enter the stables and take out horses, and in going in there to prevent it, was immediately shot down. Some few of the people of the agency escaped across the Minnesota River to Ft. Ridgely, some twelve miles east from the agency. From the agency, the Indians spread in small bands in all directions, carrying death and despair upon the unsuspecting settlers, who in most cases, not knowing the intentions of the savage murderers, allowed them to approach as usual, were shot down, tomahawked and in many cases mutilated in a most horrible manner. Others were overtaken while fleeing for safety. Their fate was the same, but more horrible, as these unfortunates knew what was coming and that they and their families were to die a most horrible death, without being able to offer any resistance or defense. Some of these unfortunates may have had some slight hope of mercy form Indians that they were personally well acquainted with, but if so, their hopes were quickly dispelled, for the savage has the mercy of the tiger of the jungle or the shark of the deep. Many hundreds died on that awful day by the hand of the savage monsters, and so the old, old story that the many must suffer to satisfy the greed of the few was once more demonstrated, for all the talk that the cause of the outbreak could not be determined, is not but "rot," pure and simple, for had the Indians been treated as agreed, honest and upright, this bloody day in the history of Minnesota would have been avoided, but as it was, the Indians never got a square deal.

The township of Milford is immediately west of New Ulm, its western line bordering the Indian reservation, and is settled mostly by Germans, a sober, industrious people, who after years of hard toil and suffering the hardships connected with the settlement of a wilderness, were now in hopes that their trouble would be about over, and better times coming, as the harvest was all that could be expected, when as a bolt of lightning from a clear sky, savage fury burst upon them. At about nine or ten o'clock on Monday, the 18th of August, 1862, a party of Indians, perhaps six or eight in number, appeared at the house of Johann Massapust, and asked for water, which was given them. The family consisted of Johann Massapust, Sr., two daughters, Maria and Julia, aged twenty and eighteen years, respectively; John Massapust, Jr., aged fifteen years; two elder boys being absent. The girls were occupied in washing dishes, the father seated nearby, John, Jr., standing near the door, when like a flash the Indians leveled their guns and fired. The girls and their father fell mortally wounded, while John, Jr., who was standing close to the Indians, was only slightly hurt from a blow with a tomahawk or hatchet, managed to run upstairs. This, of course, would not have saved him, but at the same time, two teams hauling goods from New Ulm to the Indian agency passed the road which ran only a short distance from the house, were seen by the Indians, who now made for them to kill the teamsters. This gave the boy time to escape. He ran in an opposite direction and hid in a slough, and as the house was located on a small hill, the Indians could not see him get away. When the boy left, his sister, Julia, who, although mortally wounded, had in some way managed to get outside, and seeing him run, begged him piteously to take her with him, which the poor fellow was, of course, unable to do, and despairing and half crazed, had to leave his dying sister to the tender mercy of the savage fiends. The boy, although concealed in the slough, was detected by the returning Indians and some of them made for him, when seeing this, he ran through the slough, and finding that his wet clothes hindered him in fast running, discarded his trousers, and running like a hunted animal, succeeded in his escape, thereby warning some of the settlers of the approaching danger, and saving the lives of many in the more distant parts of the town.

While some of the savages, after murdering the teamsters, returned to the house of the Massapust's the rest went to the house of a Mr. Stocker, on the opposite side of the road and bordering the timber. Mr. Stocker, who had seen the killing of the teamsters, saw the savages coming but owing to the sickness of his wife, who could not leave the bed, could not and would not leave the house, but locked the door. The Indians finding the door locked, smashed the window and one of them leveled his gun at Mrs. Stocker, when Mr. Stocker, seeing this, grabbed the gun barrel to protect his wife, and tried to wrench it from the Indian, when another of the savages took aim and killed the poor sick woman. Mr. Stocker, seeing his wife dead, and nothing more could be done in her behalf, went into the cellar, taking with him, Cecile Ochs, a girl about nine years of age, who helped at housekeeping, closing the trap door after them, while the Indians set fire to the house believing their victims would have to come out and have to be killed or be burned alive. Now, as the house had only one door and windows facing south, the savages watched that side of the house. Mr. Stocker, when in the cellar, and being certain that the house was on fire, thought of some means of escape, and seeing a small opening under the sill leading outside, tried to enlarge it. In the cellar he found some shingles, which were used for covers for milk pans, and with these dug away the earth making a passage large enough to crawl through, and as this was on the north side of the house, where the Indians (for the moment at least) did not watch, they escaped into the nearby timber and so got out of danger.

## 22. Settlers Taken by Surprise

In small bands, the Indians appeared at the several houses almost simultaneously. The families of M. Fink and Max Zeller being entirely wiped out, nobody was left to tell the story of their sad end. Florian Hartman was working in the field, when his wife came through the cornfield to bring him some refreshments, when she saw to her horror, her husband shot down, and two Indians a short distance away. As Hartman was not dead but unable to move, she ran to him and tried to drag him into a nearby cornfield, which she was unable to do, and so had to leave him to his terrible fate. The families of Casimer Herman and Athanasius Henle, seeing their nearby neighbors thus killed, had time to escape into the timber, warning Alois Palmer of the situation. They crossed the Minnesota River on Mr. Palmer's ferry and escaped to New Ulm. With Mr. Hartman, a Mr. Reiner, who helped him in harvest, was also killed. Next the house of John Zettel was visited by the savage brutes, Mr. Zettel and three or four children were killed and Mrs. Zettel left for dead. The poor woman afterward revived, and was found by a rescuing party from New Ulm later in the day. At the home of Franz Massapust a small boy was killed in the absence of his mother, who, when she returned, found the little fellow dead near the house. She with the rest of her children escaped into the nearby timber and later to New Ulm, where she was joined by her husband, who had been absent from home on that day. A Mr. Pelzl, living near the timber, was killed, also his wife. Christian Haag, seeing the home of Mr. Fink burning, mounted a horse to help them; he was met by the Indians on the road and shot down.

Next, B. Drezler was killed. Next the house of Anton Henle was visited, and the children three or four of them, killed; a little baby boy, sleeping in his cradle, received a glance blow with a hatchet; but, aside of being rudely awakened, was not much hurt. To clearly understand, what happened at this place, a little explanation is necessary; the dwellings of Anton Henle and the one of his father-in-law, Mr. Messmer, were only fifteen or twenty rods apart, but a small grove intervening, one could not be seen from the other. Mrs. Henle was about to see her mother, Mrs. Messmer on some little errand shortly before noon. She saw, when about to step out of the grove an Indian leveling his gun at her mother, and the next instant the poor woman fell, shot to death. Mrs. Henle, in deathly terror, turned to run back to her own home, when, to her horror, she saw that the savages had already entered the house. Benumbed and crazed with fear, she ran down the nearby wooded ravine, and hiding in the underbrush, did not venture out until late in the afternoon, when she heard her husband calling her name. Mr. Henle had gone to New Ulm early in the morning, intending to return soon, as it was a fine day for harvest work, and did return with a party from New Ulm, who had left the town that day for the purpose of canvassing the county in quest of volunteers to serve in the United States army, as the Civil War was then raging, and drafting was in order to bring up the quota called for by the President. This party consisted of several wagons, loaded with citizens of New Ulm, and a band of musicians, same going west, intended to make their first stop at A. Henle's place (as Mr. Henle kept a tavern) and there begin with the recruiting. About one-half mile east of the Henle place the timber fringes the road for a short distance, as a creek or ravine, draining part of the lowland, commences there. This creek crossing the road, was bridged over in a primitive way. When the first wagon approached this bridge, they were suddenly fired upon by the savages concealed in the ravine, and three of their number, Detrich, Sneider, and Fenske, were killed outright, and the rest returned as fast as possible, to New Ulm, and taking with them some wounded white settlers, Joe Messmer, who was horribly mutilated, and A. Schilling, who soon died, whom they found by the roadside. When this party reached New Ulm, Charles Roos, sheriff of Brown County, at the head of an armed detachment of citizens, proceeded at once to the place where the party had been ambushed, and from there to the place of Anton Henle, Mr. Henle being one of the party, he found his wife and his murdered children.

## 23. A Day of Terror

Before dwelling further on the doings and proceedings of this party, I will have to relate some of my own experience during that terrible Monday. In the early days, farmers, or rather the settlers, had not many acres in cultivation, so we had rented ten acres on the quarter section north of our own; the owners, two bachelors, having left the land. Mr. Anton Henle had also rented ten acres of said quarter section, twenty acres being in cultivation; our part on the northern line, Henle's south thereof. While our own land joined this to the south; Henle's place was northeast. Shortly before noon, while we were about ready with our load of wheat to take home, Mr. Messmer, father-in-law of Anton Henle, Martin, a son of Henle, and about twelve years old, and a young girl whose name I do not now remember, crossed with a load of barley close in front of our team in going home in a northern direction. Now, immediately north of where we were a range or continuation of hills (northwest to southeast), obliterated the view to the north, and Mr. Messmer, and his companions had to cross this hill in going home, so, when passing us, he remarked: "I guess this will be the last load." Of course he meant the last load before noon, but it was the last load in his life, for scarcely had they crossed said hill, when they were met by Indians and killed. We had perhaps gone ten or twelve rods in the home direction when I heard two or three shots in quick succession, and when I told Father (whose hearing was impaired), he remarked there might be some drunken Indians about, wasting their powder, so we went home, not thinking of any danger, and had our dinner. Mother said that some Indians had acted strangely, a party of four had visited the house of our neighbor south of us (Victor Zagrotzky), and had stayed there an unusually length of time, and when they left had set up a terrible howl, such as she never had heard before, and that on a hill to the east, a mounted Indian had held like a statue all morning (when we looked was just leaving, riding northward), and that about ten o'clock, a little before the Indians, a man with nothing but a shirt on had crossed the land west of us, running as fast as he could to Zagrotzky's and the Indians soon after him, but running so fast (the man with only a shirt on being John Massapust, Jr., as before mentioned) yet we did not think of any serious trouble or disturbance, and about two o'clock p.m. went for another load of wheat; we had not reached our part of the field, when Conrad Zeller, living on the southeast end on the ridge aforesaid, came running to meet us, telling us that the Indians had been killing all the neighbors and that he had carried Martin Henle (one of the party that left at the same time we did), whom the Indians had left for dead, had shown signs of life, into his house, after the Indians had left; the signs of which he bore plainly, as he was covered with blood by carrying the wounded boy. As Mr. Zeller talked very excited and in a great hurry, Father thought that some drunken Indians had perhaps committed this outrage, and so made for the house, saying to me, "take your fork and come along!" When we entered the house nobody but what seemed to be a bloody corpse was laying on a cot in the room, the family of Zeller having been in the cellar, now coming out. Martin Henle was, to all appearance, dead. Zeller now took his family to our wagon. Father, seeing a house on fire over the hill, said he would go up the hill to see what place it was, and notwithstanding Zeller's warning, went.

The next few minutes were the most exciting of my life, and I shall not forget them to my last day. Father had gone but a short distance, when suddenly, out of the timber, not far to the northeast of us, about a dozen Indians, all mounted, came galloping along the road. As soon as I saw them I recalled Father, and, as he was hard of hearing, I had to call rather loud. The Indians, hearing me before Father did, all halted and looked our way. Father, now seeing the Indians and now being convinced that something serious was going on, told me to stay where I was and watch the Indians, and should they come our way, hide in the slough nearby or in the cellar, so that at least one of us might be saved. He would try to reach home and help mother and the little ones, but, should the Indians come our way, he would have no show in reaching home. My protest did no good. Zeller, by this time had, with his family, reached our team, and, as Father joined them, they drove away as fast as an ox-team will go, and as the hill was between them and the savages, could not be seen by the latter who, after having stopped at the place mentioned before, a short time, rode on along the road facing south. Now was the time when it soon must decide where they would go. At the place where the road branched off to the west, they halted a few moments, looking toward the Zeller house; then following the main road to the corner where it turns sharply eastward, and, following the road east were met by another party of Indians, and when these two parties of savages met, halted there for some time, and I made for home in a three-mile-a-minute gait and reached home a little later than the ox-team, and after the Indians were out of sight we left for New Ulm. While I was alone at the Zeller house, watching, I saw the supposed dead boy, Martin Henle, move his hands. I called him by name, but received no answer. When we were about to leave, Victor Zagrotzky, our next neighbor to the south of us, was seen running aimlessly to and fro on the prairie, so I went to him to tell what was up, when he told me that he had been to town and heard of the outbreak, and on coming to his house found windows smashed, bedding outside and ripped open, and dared not go inside for fear to see his family butchered and mutilated. He of course did not know that they had been warned in time by the Massapust boy, and had escaped just in time to a settlement a little farther south, where people had gathered in considerable numbers, so when the four Indians who had followed them appeared upon the scene, they did not dare to attack, but went further southward, and the party of whites reached New Ulm in safety.

When we got about half way to New Ulm, Zagrotzky, who had followed, implored and begged piteously that some one should go back with him to search for his family, which had gone with the party before mentioned, a different road to New Ulm, but of course he could not know that. As our party now had been augmented by two teams; the families of H. Albrecht and Anton Ochs, and as from now on the road was deemed safe, Father, with Mr. Zeller and Mr. Zagrotzky, went to search for the latter's family, and for the purpose of looking after Martin Henle. The chances, of course, were that they might meet Indians and be killed, but they went. They reached their destination without seeing any Indians. After searching for the family of Zagrotzky, which could not be found, they went to the house of Mr. Zeller, and when entering, seeing the boy who was believed to be dead, looking at them and trying to smile. They brought him water, which he eagerly drank, but they found it impossible to remove him, as there was no team to be had. When they saw, in the direction of the Henle place, a considerable number of people on the road, and after looking for a short time, could be distinguished to be white men, Mr. Zeller went to them to inform them of the fate of Martin Henle, while Father remained. In a short time some of the party, among them Mr. Henle himself, appeared, and the poor boy was once more untied with his grief-stricken parents. This was the party under Sheriff Roos which arrived with the wounded they had rescued; among them Mrs. Zettel, at New Ulm at about ten o'clock in the evening. Mrs. Zettel and Martin Henle both died about two weeks afterward, and so, all in all, thirty-five men, women and children were murdered, in this immediate neighborhood on that never-to-be-forgotten bloody Monday.

## 24. Theresa Henle's Account

There is still residing in New Ulm a lady who tells the story of what she saw and endured at the hands of the redskins in the memorable month of August, 1862. Mrs. Theresa Henle, wife of Anton Henle, into whose house the citizens of New Ulm intended to go when they were attacked on their way. This is Mrs. Henle's account of the affair as witnessed by herself:

"My husband, Anton Henle, went to New Ulm on the 18th of August, intending to return soon to haul in some wheat, because it was a very fine day. Besides running a farm we kept a sort of a stopping place for travelers. A Frenchman who had remained overnight left our house at 9 o'clock, intending to go to the Lower Agency, a distance of about twenty miles. Several men who were hauling freight for him to that place had left our house earlier. Nothing extraordinary happened except that at ten o'clock, the Frenchman returned and drove toward New Ulm as fast as he could go. It was very strange to see him thus pass our place without even a single look toward it, since he was never known to pass without calling in. Toward noon I went to my mother who lived near us, to get some lettuce. On returning home, I saw three naked Indians and went back to warn mother. I found her in the garden. As soon as I approached her she was shot, and falling down, she cried aloud: 'O, Theresa!' Seized with terror I ran toward my house, fearing for my children. I found three Indians in the house. One of them jumped at me, but I ran down the incline into the woods which was only a little way off. There I stood for a while not knowing what to do. I understood now why the Frenchman had returned in such great haste. Filled with a desire to at least save my baby, I went back toward the house, but noticed too many Indians around to do anything. Then I went to a neighbor, Benedict Drexler, whose house was about thirty rods from ours. I went in through the window and found no one at home. Later on, Drexler was found beheaded in the field. His wife and children were in the cornfield. The Indians shot at her but she fled. When I heard the shooting I ran into the woods in order to get back to Mother, but saw a large number of Indians who were putting up a red and white flag. I turned back again into the woods and remained in the dry bed of a creek, from which place I could hear the rattling of the wagons coming from New Ulm, and also the shots that were fired at them by the Indians, because I was hardly five hundred steps from the place where the Indians were lying in ambush. I remained there, tortured with the most terrible thoughts about my husband and children, which troubled me more than my own misery. Whilst sitting there, neglected and forlorn, my two dogs came up to me trembling. Toward evening I heard the voice of my husband in the direction of the house calling me, and I came forth from my hiding place."

Anton Henle also wanted to get to his place with the recruiting party, but he had to return to New Ulm, as has been related. When toward evening a volunteer company which had been organized at New Ulm went out to protect and assist the settlers, Henle was among the number. He did not expect to find a member of his family alive. In his house there reigned the supreme silence of death, and nothing but destruction was visible. What joy must have filled his heart when he heard the voice of his wife in response to his pitiful cries! One of his children, a girl of four, they found dead, and a servant girl of eighteen, beheaded. A child eight years old, who had been with its grandmother, was found dead without any wound; the child probably died of fright. One of his boys, Martin, a lad twelve years old, was found by Conrad Zeller. He had seventeen wounds upon his body, but was still alive. He died two weeks later.

This boy related that when he was running away a mounted Indian kept galloping at his side, striking him with a tomahawk, until at last, being completely exhausted by pain and loss of blood, he fell to the ground; and the Indian, believing him to be dead, rode away.

The number of Henle's relatives killed on that awful day amounted to twenty-one. Among them were: Martin Fink and wife, Monica; Max Fink and his nephew; Martin Merkle; Max Zeller and wife, Lucretia; daughter of Martin Fin, and their four children; John and Barbara Zettel and their four children; Anton and Mary Ann Messmer; Anton Henle's children, Martin, Anton, and Mary, and also Florian Hartman, brother-in-law of the Henle's.

## 25. A Thrilling Experience

Among the scores of thrilling experiences connected with the never-to-be-forgotten massacre, is one told by Mrs. Maria Hartman-Bobleter, whose first husband, Florian Hartman, was killed by the Indians. Her story, as related several years ago, is as follows:

"My husband, Florian Hartman, was on the 18th of August engaged with another man, John Rohner, in binding wheat near our house. When I had their dinner ready for them I heard some noise, and on looking out I could see houses on fire, and also thought I could see them at work trying to save the buildings. At the same moment I heard a cry "Nippo!"(kill) and the reports of several rifles. Thinking the Indians were killing some cattle, I ran out to see what was going on. An Indian came close up to the house, stared at me and then ran away. Full of fear I hurried toward my husband who was about forty rods from the house, and on crossing the road I noticed a man lying on the ground and thought he was asleep. It was Hartman's hired man, Rhoner, and he was covered with blood. Looking for my husband I found him about thirty steps away from Rhoner, lying on the ground. He motioned me to keep quiet and to drag him into the cornfield, because he was shot. Stricken with fear, I was powerless to do it. I cast myself down beside my husband, and in my excessive grief knew not what to do. Soon after, two Indians came up to the dying Rhoner and fired two more shots at him. My poor husband then begged me to hide in the cornfield, because I could not do him any good where I was. I ran and hid as he told me, digging a hole in the ground with my hands to creep into. I remained there till toward evening. Two Indians passed close by me, but did not notice me.

"About eight o'clock I heard some one weeping bitterly, but did not dare to leave my place, thinking it might be an Indian. After a while I crept toward my husband, and found him cold and stiff in death. I took some hair from his head as a remembrance, and fled into the woods. Even the animals seemed to realize what was going on. Under a large oak, in the vicinity of a spring, I remained all night, and toward four o'clock in the morning I hurried toward the Minnesota in order to escape across the ferry into Nicollet County. But the boat was on the other side of the river. I tried in vain to get across on the rope, and so I had to hide all day in the woods, and suffered greatly from the mosquitoes. About eight o'clock in the evening I went back to our house and passed five Indian tepees on my way. I went into the house to take some clothing, and in picking up some of the bedding that was lying on the floor I noticed a wounded Indian lying thereon, and immediately ran away. When I passed the barn in my flight an Indian fired at me, but missed me on account of the darkness of the night. During the whole of that night and the following day I remained in concealment. On the fourth day it rained heavily. I was very tired and completely worn out. Such sadness overcame me that I was almost sorry for not having found death at the hands of the Indians. The rain continued to the fifth day, and being completely drenched, I ventured back to the house; but on going in I found everything gone. However, I felt happy to find some dry underclothing to put on. The hogs were in the pen and screaming from hunger. I had compassion on them and gave them some corn. I was lucky enough to find a loaf of bread, and with this I went back to my hiding place. But I was sorry to have betrayed my presence through my compassion for hungry animals. On the sixth day I wanted to go to the house, but noticing some Indians near the place I hurried back. During this and the next day I heard continual shooting. On the evening of the eighth day my dog came to me and was overjoyed to see me. I, too, rejoiced as if I had met with a friend in my terrible loneliness. I shared the remainder of my bread with him. He seemed to be very hungry. But at the same moment the thought struck me that he might betray my hiding place and in order to remove that danger I took my apron and strangled him with it. But he fought so fiercely, that it was with the greatest exertions that I succeeded in killing him.

"On the morning of the ninth day I heard a great noise which seemed to come nearer and nearer; but I soon felt relieved when I found it to be only a few hogs. I remained two more days in my concealment, and hardly dared to go a hundred steps farther. In my terrible condition, living on a little bread and wild berries, life seemed to have new charms. I enjoyed the singing of the birds, and thanked my Creator and prayed for the preservation of my life.

"A strange presentiment made me leave my hiding place on the twelfth day. I went to the homes of my brothers, and to that of Cassimir, but found them all empty. A terrible sight presented itself to me in Zettel's house.

There I found the bodies of the father and his four children, and between them was a loaf of bread. I was very hungry and greatly desired to take the bread, but the odor of the corpses was so repulsive that I could not eat it. In Pelzyls' house I found the dead bodies of his father and of a woman. A short distance from the house I found the bodies of old Messmer and of a girl. In Anton Henle's house lay the body of one of the children. The air was everywhere filled with the stench of the corpses.

"I now determined to go to New Ulm, six miles distant. In the cemetery I noticed a white flag, which filled me with courage and hope. But when I came near town and noticed that many buildings had been burned down and the town was deserted, new fear and anxiety came over me. I did not go farther, but returned immediately to my hiding place because I was afraid I might meet Indians in town. At seven o'clock in the evening I was again at my brother Anton's house, from which I could hear a great noise. I went in because I thought I would have to die anyhow. The noise, however, was caused by all sorts of animals that had gathered in the house.

"From there I went to my own house, and to bed, and reproached myself for having gone so far. On the following day I searched for some potatoes; but it was only with great difficulty, and after going to two other houses, that I could find a match. As soon as I had found some matches I returned to my house, feeling rich and happy, and prepared a soup. I had two matches left, and for fear that I might lose them I kept up a fire at a stump nearby.

"On the fourteenth day I found some eggs and a sack of flour, but could not make use of the flour. After that I remained indoors most of the time. An ox came up to the house with an ugly wound. I washed the wound and the animal got well. A calf had one of its eyes shot out but it got well. I then began to gather plums and nuts and dig potatoes, because I had lost all hope of being rescued, and wanted to provide for the winter. I was under the impression that all the settlers had been put to death.

"On the seventeenth day I went to look for the body of my husband, and, on my way thither, I heard some shooting and the barking of dogs. I almost fainted on looking up and seeing eight men coming toward me. One of them leveled his gun, and now I thought I would after all have to die. But the cry, "Oh, sister!" roused me again, and in a moment I was in the arms of my brother, Athanasius, who had taken me for a squaw on account of the changes made by my sufferings and anxieties. Fortunately, I knew of an old wagon nearby which had been left my the Indians. My brother had only a sled for his horse. The wagon was fixed up and he went to town in it, where I again enjoyed the society of human beings, of which I had been deprived for more than a fortnight."

## 26. Thrilling Incidents of the Battle of New Ulm

Buck in his Indian Outbreaks–a work published in 1904–says: "the Indian War of 1862 developed as much as genuine bravery and true heroism on the part of the whites as any war that ever took place. Numerous were the acts of bravery at the battle of New Ulm, only a few of which can here be mentioned. Specifically, I can mention that of J. B. Trogdon, first. He was my friend and client, living on a claim below New Ulm, and knew the Indian character well. A braver man never lived. He was an old bachelor, without relatives in this state, so far as I know. After the battle I saw him on his noble steed, and with his long curly hair thrown back over his shoulders and floating in the wind, and his trusty rifle resting on the shoulders of his faithful horse, he was the picture of a Spartan hero who knew no such word as cowardice. Bryant, in his history, says of him:

"At another time, J. B. Trogdon, in company with Captain Potter, rode to a point of timber in the rear of the town, where they saw an Indian drop down in the grass, and another on a horse, a short distance behind. In order to avoid a shot from the Indian in the grass, and at the same time get a shot at the mounted warrior, it was suggested that Trogdon ride around and come up the hill from the ravine, and thus get near the savage without being observed. Trogdon immediately proceeded to put the suggestion into execution; but as he approached near enough to fire, twenty mounted Indians made a dash after him, with a devilish yell, and endeavored to cut him off from the town by running him into a slough. Then followed a scene of the wildest excitement. The mettle of the steeds was put to a test. At one time, in rounding the slough, it was thought Trogdon would be cut off; but a yell from him gave his splendid charger increased speed, and he distanced the Indians twenty yards. As he came near our lines, twenty shots were fired at him, but the aim was too high, and the balls had passed over his head. He immediately wheeled and discharged his Sharp's rifle at his pursuers, but without effect; and after passing within our lines, Trogdon again wheeled his horse, rode out toward the foe in easy rifle range, and fired deliberately at his pursuers, while over twenty rifle balls aimed at him, fell harmless at his feet, or passed over his head.'

"Brave Trogdon, with all his faults and life's failure, I gladly bear this token of personal friendship and respect for one of the bravest spirits that passed through the trying ordeal of Indian outbreak of 1862.

"In the battle of Saturday the savages got possession of a building from which it was necessary to dislodge them. The Hon. D. G. Shillock, then a practicing lawyer at New Ulm, called for volunteers to do this, and started with several men to the building. Before reaching it the others fell back, but he with his perseverance and brave heart reached the building, and with his unerring rifle cleared it of its savage occupants without being injured, though subsequently he received a severe wound in the knee which maimed him for life.

"Another brave man was Nehemiah S. Burgess, who performed an act of valor unsurpassed in all the deadly conflicts of nations or individuals. Upon this subject Judson Jones, an early settler of Minnesota, now living at Cleveland, LeSueur County, sends me the following communication: 'There is one unmentioned name which ought to be rescued from oblivion before those who were in the battle of New Ulm and know the facts pass away, ant that is the name of Nehemiah S. Burgess, of Altona, LeSueur County who did the bravest deed at New Ulm. At the most critical period of the defense, when the besiegers were in full force, and the besieged were all hidden within the barricades from the murderous fire of the foe, two buildings remained unburned outside the barricaded street. It was feared that they would be taken possession of by the Indians in the night, which would enfilade the barricaded street and thus render the defense hopeless. It was a case of life or death. Those buildings must be burned, and a call was made for someone to volunteer for the forlorn hope. Among all these brave men no one answered the call. It seemed sure death, for the open ground to be crossed to reach the buildings was an easy range for the enemies' bullets and how was escape possible? At last a man, Nehemiah S. Burgess, stepped out and said, 'I will go,' and, preparing his kindlings, he ventured forth. As soon as he appeared outside the barricades the Indians opened fire, the bullets falling around him like hail-stones until he disappeared behind the buildings. On his way back, after firing the buildings, the same fire assailed him. When safe inside the barricades he turned to look, expecting to see the buildings all in flames; but the buildings were wet with recent rains, and the fire had gone out.

Undismayed, he prepared another lot of kindling and crossed the gulf of hell. This time he waited until he saw the buildings wrapped in flames, and again returned through the relentless fire of the foe unhurt. Major Buell, of St. Peter, who was an eye-witness, gave me the account of it soon after the arrival of the refugees at St. Peter, adding: 'It was the bravest thing I saw done at New Ulm.' Mr. Burgess also told me of it, adding, 'I never expected to get back alive, so I took a last look at the sun, and prayed God to take care of Margaret and the children.' It was he also who led in Flandrau's charge, and received the bullet through his right arm. It was while this would was being dressed that he told me the story. Mr. Burgess is an old man now (1891), eighty-eight years of age, but has many warm friends among the heroes of New Ulm, and this tribute is his just due. It will be read with pleasure by his children and his children's children. God bless the old heroes!

(Signed) JUDSON JONES

"And the name of Capt. William Bierbauer stands high on the scroll of the brave and heroic defenders of New Ulm. When he heard of the Indian outbreak he immediately raised a company in Mankato, and, as its captain, proceeded to New Ulm, where he rendered valiant service through the siege. Judge Flandrau says to him: 'Captain Bierbauer and his gallant company were very prominent figures at the battle of New Ulm, which was fought on August 23, 1862. The bravery of Captain Bierbauer was most conspicuous, and produced the best result. During the critical period of the fight, when bullets were falling fast and thick from the Sioux rifles, I noticed one man standing alone and in advance of all others, firing at the Indians, and manfully maintaining his position. We advanced and ascertained that it was Captain Bierbauer of Mankato, and directing the attention of the men to this manifestation of bravery, they rallied to assist in maintaining the position held by the captain. I shall never forget the effect it produced on these men who had been on the run a moment before. When they recognized their captain in this exposed position, so coolly holding his own, the effect was electrical. The state of Minnesota owes Captain Bierbauer a debt of gratitude and will ever keep his memory green.

"The name of Dr. A. W. Daniels should not be forgotten. While the battle was raging the hottest, leaving to Doctors McMahon, Mayo and Ayers the care of the wounded, he seized his gun, and a participant in the battle by his side says that among the brave, none were braver. His elder brother, Dr. Jared W. Daniels, was one of the heroes of the battle of Birch Coulee."

## 27. Reminiscences of the Little Crow Uprising[12]

Considering the two thousand lives involved, largely women and children, the successful defense of New Ulm was the most momentous event in the Indian War of 1862-63. From that defeat the Indians turned westward and abandoned further combined raids upon the settlements. The active part taken by the people of St. Peter will ever be an impressive chapter in the eventful history of that city. Her immediate and generous response with volunteers, and their long and hurried march, enabled them to join in defending New Ulm in the afternoon, and later to participate in the uncertain issue of battle that held the besieged in its grasp for a whole day. The command of General Sibley would have reached the city too late to save it from savage fury, and had not the response been immediate from St. Peter, LeSueur and Mankato, its fate must have been horrible to contemplate.

Some of the events of that battle have never been fully stated in the official reports, and others not mentioned came under the observation of the writer. Therefore it will be of interest to learn, from one who had superior opportunities, the particulars of the battle as seen by him.

The news of the Indian outbreak reached St. Peter during the night of Monday, the 18th of August, 1862, it having commenced at the lower Sioux agency at seven o'clock that morning. Major Galbraith, who had reached St. Peter in the evening before, on his way to Ft. Snelling with a company of recruits, learning of the situation, at daylight started on his return to Ft. Ridgely, which he reached in time to participate in its defense.

At four o'clock in the morning of Tuesday the writer was notified of the outbreak and was asked by Captain Dodd to go to Rounseville and Briggs neighborhood, six miles to the northwest, and notify the settlers, and he informed me at that time that messengers had already been dispatched in other directions. I was soon on the way, going from house to house, spreading the alarm, and sending others to more distant locations. On my return the refugees were already pouring in, and by noon the village

---

[12] By Dr. Asa W. Daniels, in a paper read before the executive council, November 14, 1910, and now forming a part of the records of the Minnesota Historical Society collections, volume XV, 1915.

became crowded with men, women and children. Some had been attacked on the way, and bore their wounded with them. All were in a most pitiable condition, having in their fright and haste taken little clothing and no provisions, reaching their destination completely destitute. Every house was sympathetically thrown open to the refugees, and was soon filled from cellar to garret. The vacant Ewing House, a hotel of fifty rooms or more, and an unoccupied store building, were soon filled, and being of stone afforded safety and comparative comfort; but many were compelled to resort to sheds and barns, or to remain unsheltered for some nights, until better provided.

## A Year Before the Outbreak

A little more than a year before the outbreak I had located in St. Peter, having left the government service at the lower Agency, as a physician and surgeon to the Sioux Indians, after a service of more than seven years. I had visited them a month before and heard from them many complaints, principally against their physician, Doctor Humphry. My long service among them had been satisfactory to myself and the Indians, and I had many warm friends in every band, among them being Little Crow, and I may say most of the chiefs. Therefore, when the news of the outbreak came, I was in great doubt in regard to its being general, but thought it confined to a single band, and that the outrages had occurred when they were under the influence of whisky sold them by the whites. But within twenty-four hours my confidence in my old friends was rudely shattered, and I came to realize, on seeing the dead and wounded, that the outbreak was general and of the most barbarous character.

As a government officer, I had observed for more than two years the close intimacy that was growing up between the Sioux and Winnebagoes. This was apparent from frequent visits of large parties of Winnebagoes to the agency, intermarriages that took place, uniting in games, and tribal pledges of friendship. No doubt some of the Winnebagoes participated in the battle that took place, but were to discreet to have it known. Had success attended the Sioux at Ft. Ridgely and New Ulm, there is little doubt there would have been a union of the tribes against the whites.

At St. Peter, to which we returned after a slight digression, Captain Dodd and Major Flandrau had enlisted about one hundred and forty men to march at once in defense of New Ulm. Many of these volunteers fled from their country homes in the morning, hurriedly disposed of their families, and bravely responded to the call for a thirty-mile march before the close of their eventful day.

I joined them as a surgeon of the command, and we were on our way about midday. The men were armed with double-barreled shotguns, a few rifles, and some other arms of uncertain efficiency. Some were on horseback, and a few in buggies; having to carry my surgical and medical cases, I availed myself of the latter conveyance. On reaching Courtland, twenty miles, a heavy shower drenched the command, but the march was continued, all being enthusiastic to reach New Ulm, where refugees informed me, there was a little battle going on and much of the town burned. We reached Redstone, two miles form the village just as it was getting dark, and from that distance it did look as if the whole town was on fire; but crossing the ferry, we rushed on and reached the vicinity of the Dakota House about ten o'clock at night.

As we were leaving St. Peter we were joined by the command under Captain Tousley, of LeSueur, of nearly one hundred men, who continued with us on the march to New Ulm. With them, as surgeons, were Dr. Otis Ayers and Dr. William W. Mayo, father of the two distinguished surgeons at Rochester. It was midnight before we found quarters for the night, and then I shared my bed with Doctor Ayers, passing a comfortable night after a long and strenuous day.

## SITUATION AT NEW ULM

Early in the morning of Wednesday we were looking over the situation as left from the engagement the afternoon before. On a vacant lot near the center of town lay six dead, brought in from the scene of the engagement, and others had been cared for by their families. The physicians then visited the wounded and cared for them, and for some of the refugees who were ill from fright and anxiety.

During the forenoon of Wednesday, Captain Bierbauer came in with nearly one hundred men from Mankato, and a few men came from Nicollet, under the command of Capt. Samuel Coffin. An organization was formed on that day by the military, who selected Major Flandrau as commander, Captain Dodd as lieutenant, and S. A. Buell as provost marshal. Pickets were established on the outskirts of the town, and guard duty for the night. During the day quarters and the commissary departments were established for the different commands.

A company of sixteen mounted men from St. Peter, among them Henry A. Swift and Horace Austin, afterwards governor of the state, had started to the front some hours before the command of Flandrau was ready to leave, and had reached New Ulm in time to participate in the battle of Tuesday afternoon.

Thursday morning, after guard mount and after a company had been elected to dig rifle pits, a company of a hundred men, under the command of Captain Dodd, was ordered to go the Little Cottonwood settlement, six miles south, to bury the dead and rescue any that might be hiding or wounded. Dr. Ayers and myself were detailed to accompany the command. The doctor invited me to have a seat with him in his buckboard, which I thankfully accepted. The command had hardly made half the distance to the settlement before they were fired upon from ambush, but none was wounded, and, after returning the volley, we continued our march. Three mounted Indians soon showed themselves, but at a safe distance, observing our course, and in derision waving their blankets, keeping in sight most of the time during the march..

On reaching the settlement, the saddest scene presented itself that humanity is ever called upon to witness. The massacre had probably taken place on Monday before, and the dead were lying in all directions about the farm houses—in bed, in different rooms of the house, in the yard, near the grain stacks, and on the lawn. During the three days that the remains had been exposed the flies had done their work, and as a result the faces of the dead presented a revolting spectacle. Trenches were dug, and the bodies were gathered together and laid within, blankets were spread over them, and a prayer was offered; then earth to earth, ashes to ashes, and the command turned sadly away, having witnessed a burial scene that could never be forgotten.

By military the day had been passed in strengthening the defenses of the town, providing themselves with ammunition, and fixing upon positions of advantage in case of an attack. News came in during the day of fighting at Ft. Ridgely, and of Captain Marsh's defeat at the agency, and many other alarming accounts from refugees.

## A LONG AND USELESS MARCH.

The principal event of Friday was the detailing of one hundred and forty men, under command of Captain Tousley, to go to Leavenworth, west and south of Ft. Ridgely, expecting to find persons there unable to escape and that might be rescued, but nothing definite was known in regard to the situation there. Doctors Ayers, Mayo and myself joined the command–I again having a seat with Doctor Ayers. The route was across an open prairie, and we had not proceeded far before we discovered three mounted Indian scouts to the north keeping in line with us and watching our course. Late in the afternoon we reached the vicinity of Ft. Ridgely and for the first time heard cannonading going on there, the sounds reaching us at short intervals. After its significance had fully impressed me, I said to Doctor Ayers that the Indians have attacked the fort in great force, and that as scouts had been watching our course, in case we continued our march to Leavenworth they would certainly withdraw from the fort during the afternoon or in the morning and cut us off. We had expected to remain at Leavenworth over night, returning the next day. Doctor Ayers agreed with me fully, and rode forward and consulted with Captain Tousley, who called a halt and gave his reasons for so doing, asking of the command to express their wishes by a showing of hands. It was carried by those in favor of going forward by two or three votes.

We continued our march for another hour, the warning notes of cannon coming to us regularly; the sun was nearly down, night was coming on, and fatigue was telling upon the command, when a second halt was called and another vote was taken, which resulted in an order to return to New Ulm. We reached our return destination after midnight, thoroughly worn out and disgusted from this long and useless march, which might have resulted not only in the destruction of the command, but perhaps in the capture of New Ulm.

The morning of Saturday was warm and fair, and at first we hopefully looked forward to an uneventful day. Much time had been taken in preparing for an attack, by burning outer buildings, digging rifle-pits, and loop-holing such walls as might be made serviceable. On that morning

Colonel Flandrau gave me a dozen men and I barricaded the avenue a little west of the Gross hotel. From the roof of the Erd building, a central business block, with a glass an extensive view was had of the surrounding country, and at this point of observation a watchman was on duty during the day.

### The Attack Begins

The first surprise and alarm of the morning came when a guard mount, west of the town, Lieutenant Edwards was instantly killed by an Indian so concealed in the grass that danger was unsuspected. About eight o'clock a.m., the watchman from the roof saw Indians collecting some two miles west of town, and signal smokes from the northwest. His observations were confirmed by officers and others. The certainty of a deadly conflict with a barbarous foe, when no quarter is expected is a most trying test of courage, but, with few exceptions, the situation was heroically accepted. The women and children were hurried to places of safety, the command was got under arms, and the physicians selected rooms for receiving the wounded, Doctors Mayo and McMahon in the Dakota House, and Doctor Ayers and myself in a store room on the opposite side of the avenue.

Within one hour the large body of Indians who had been forming on the west, were seen to be rapidly moving upon the town. The signals indicated a like approach, Colonel Flandrau posted his men upon the slope of one of the terraces on the west with a line of skirmishes in front. Little Crow was mounted and led his warriors, who were on foot. In a long line with flanks curved forward, they approached in silence within a quarter of a mile of the defenders, when they gave a terrific war-cry and rushed forward upon a run, holding their fire until they had received that of our men, and then delivering an effective volley at close range. The defenders fell back in panic and the whole line retreated to the barricades. The assault was well executed, and had it been pushed to its limit might have resulted in the capture of the town by the Indians. But our men soon rallied behind the barricades and buildings, which arrested the onward rush of the Indians and compelled them to seek protection of the outer buildings.

Lieutenant Huey, with seventy-five men, was ordered to the ferry to prevent the Indians from crossing from the north side. Either from a misunderstanding or over-confidence, he crossed his command to the north side of the river, there meeting a large body of the enemy, retreated to Nicollet, and was not seen again until the next day. This unfortunate event was a serious loss to the defense. The firing from both sides became rapid, sharp and general, the Indians gradually pushing their way in surrounding the town, which they accomplished before midday. They fought with the utmost boldness and ferocity, and with the utmost skill and caution from every hollow and grass patch, and from behind every house and hillock or log. The crisis came at two p.m., when the Indians fired buildings on both sides of the avenue in the lower part of town. A strong wind was blowing from the east, and the conflagration threatened the destruction of our only defense. Colonel Frandrau rallied a sufficient force, and charging down the street, drove the enemy from the avenue. But just at this critical time the wind changed to the opposite direction, and clouds, which had been gathering for hours, shed upon our threatened locality a sufficient shower of rain to prevent the further extending of the flames.

### Death of Captain Dodd

The unfortunate incident of the day's battle that led to the death of Captain Dodd has never been correctly reported. In justice to the brave men that participated in that critical movement, a correct understanding should be had of the reasons that, at the time, seemed to make the undertaking imperative.

It will be remembered that Lieutenant Huey had retreated toward Nicollet in the morning, and all through the day we looked for his return with reinforcements, which really took place the following day.

About five o'clock there appeared beyond the Indian outer line, at the east, some forty or fifty men, marching in single file, under the command of an officer, carrying the American flag. They were dressed in citizens' clothes, and all had the appearance of the reinforcements so anxiously expected.

The Indians had again gained possession of the buildings on the avenue east, perhaps five blocks from the Dakota House, and from that position were delivering a galling fire upon our line.

Immediately, on discovering what all thought to be our reinforcements, Captain Dodd, in a short speech, volunteered to lead any that would follow to the clearing of the avenue of the Indians and joining our reinforcements beyond. Rev. Father Sunrisen and Doctor Mayo both made speeches urging all to unite in support of Dodd. Some twenty men responded, Dodd and Shoemaker being mounted, and proceeded down the avenue. It was a movement of only a few moments consideration, and seemed to promise an important result. Dodd rushed forward with a cheer, hardly coming within the Indian lines before receiving a deadly volley, which hurriedly sent them back to positions of safety. Captain Dodd wheeled his horse and reached a log blacksmith's shop, when the horse plunged forward and fell. Partially supporting himself and being assisted by others, the fatally-wounded leader was taken to the building, a cot prepared and there within an hour he died. He had received three mortal wounds, two other slight wounds, and the horses ridden by Dodd and Shoemaker were both killed. The writer had witnessed from our hospital the whole movement, saw Dodd fall and hurried to his assistance. There was little that could be done, as he was in a dying condition. He appreciated his condition and met it courageously, giving a message to his wife and to Bishop Whipple, with the utmost coolness and consideration.

## An Indian Stratagem

The party we had supposed to be reinforcements, upon the volley from the Indians and our men falling back, suddenly disappeared, and it proved to be a stratagem to draw out some of our men and cut them off. Had the Indians in the buildings held their fire until they had advanced a half block further, it would have been successful. In explanation of how the Indians became possessed of so many suits of citizens' clothes, it may be said that twenty-two months before one hundred and fifty suits were issued to them by the government, under the pledge of becoming farmers, much of this clothing having never been worn more than a few days.

The assault commencing in the morning at 9:30, was kept up without interruption until dark, when the Indians withdrew in the direction of Ft. Ridgely. During the evening all buildings outside of our barricades were burned. By ourselves and the Indians one hundred and ninety buildings were destroyed. We lost ten killed and forty wounded, the small loss being accounted for by the fact that we were fighting from the loop-holes of buildings and barricades. The Indian loss has never been known. Both hospitals received and dress the wounded, providing temporary cots for them. Some that were only slightly wounded returned and continued in the fight during the day.

Saturday night was anxious and disturbed with desultory firing by our guards, and perhaps by the Indians. Sunday morning it seemed from heavy firing that the assault was to be renewed; but it gradually lessened and by noon ceased entirely. About noon Capt. E. St. Julien Cox arrived with about fifty men, accompanied by Lieutenant Huey with part of his detachment which had been cut off the day before. During Sunday afternoon search was made for the recovery of the dead. Three or four were found that had fallen so far out as to be exposed to any indignity that the Indians might offer, but none was scalped or otherwise mutilated. Jerry Quane, a St. Peter volunteer, had the totem of Little Crow attached to the clothing over his breast. The totem was the skin of a crow, preserved in its natural form, symbolic of the family name. The parting with such a treasured emblem was to boastfully inform us from whom the brave defender had met his death.

## RETREAT TO MANKATO

Early on Monday morning the order was issued for the evacuation of the village. Colonel Flandrau must have been wholly responsible for this move, as I am sure the medical officers were not consulted and were entirely ignorant of it until a short time before the movement was commenced. We had received reinforcements the day before, our position was stronger than ever, the sanitary conditions did not necessitate great urgency in moving, and the volunteers would have loyally remained. General Sibley was at St. Peter, and would have arrived within a few days, therefore it was a mistake to retreat from New Ulm until relieved by him. The route was part of the way through a dense forest, and had a few Indians attacked a panic and massacre would have ensued. It is an ungracious and unwelcome task to criticize the colonel, but a truthful statement seems to demand that it should be done, in this respect at least. Nearly two thousand men, women and children took up the march for Mankato, thirty miles distant, bearing the wounded in conveyances. Fortunately the long march was uneventful, and we reached our destination late in the evening, where we received a generous reception.

On Tuesday the volunteers from St. Peter reached home and disbanded. The writer brought with him the Rev. Mr. Saunders, severely wounded, who had volunteered with the LeSueur company. Some of the wounded were left at Mankato, but most of them came to St. Peter, and their care became most urgent. My brother, assistant surgeon with General Sibley's command, assisting, we established a hospital in the court room at the court house. The room was large, well ventilated and afforded space for twenty beds, sufficient for the most serious cases. The care of the hospital devolved upon me, as my brother left with his command two or three days later.

Of the cases that came under my care, the most serious were as follows: Mr. Summers, of Nicollet, shot through the spinal column, died.; Rufus Huggins was shot through the mouth, severing his tongue, recovered; a Sibley County volunteer, with a compound fracture of the arm bone near the shoulder joint, had amputation and recovered; Rev. Mr. Saunders, with an abdominal wound, recovered; Mr. Bean, a St. Peter volunteer, with a shot through the face, fracturing his lower jaw, recovered; a St. Paul volunteer, with a penetrating gunshot wound of the brain, lived two or three days and died insane at St. Peter.

From the time the news of the outbreak was received, the citizens of St. Peter were active in providing for the refugees and the protection of the city. They organized committees for the various duties, as care for the sick, supplying food and clothing and fortifying. Night and day guard duty was kept up, earth-works were thrown up, rifle-pits and barricades erected.

## THE GOVERNMENT NOT GUILTLESS

In closing this paper the writer, who was so long and intimately associated with the Indians as a government official, desires to say that he found this people possessed of many of the virtues common to the human family, and that socially and morally their lives were of a standard quite as high as among civilized races. The outbreak was induced by long-continued violation of treaty obligations on the part of the government, inflicting upon these unfortunate wards untold want and suffering. Like violent acts of mobs among civilized communities, the massacre was a barbarous and unreasoning protest against injustice. Had the government faithfully carried out the treaty obligations and dealt with the Sioux justly and humanely, the outbreak would not have occurred.

# IV. Punishment of the Sioux

## 28. Introduction

The Indians were defeated—they lost all the twenty-mile wide and one-hundred-mile-long strip of land reserved for them along the Minnesota River above New Ulm to the headwaters, having it abrogated by the United States government on account of this war, which was contrary to the treaty terms made at Traverse des Sioux in 1851. They also had thirty-eight of their leaders in the bloody massacre hanged at Mankato, December 26, 1862. And they were as a people driven from the state forever.

This execution was brought about in the following manner: After the campaign of 1862, and the guilty parties were confined at Camp Lincoln, near Mendota, the idea of executing capitally three hundred Indians aroused the sympathy of those far removed from these scenes of butchery. President Abraham Lincoln was importuned, principally by the people of the East and the Quakers in Pennsylvania. The voice of the blood of innocence crying from the ground, the wailings of mothers bereft of their children were hushed in the tender cry of sympathy for the condemned. Even the Christian ministers, stern in the belief that "Whosoever sheddith man's blood by man shall his blood be shed," seemed now the most zealous for the pardon of these merciless outlaws who had shed the blood of innocent women and children in the time of peace.

Senators Wilkinson and William Windom made eloquent, urging appeals to the President for the proper execution of sentence in the case of these Indians. One quotation from one of these distinguished statesmen's address is sufficient to show the trend of sentiment in Minnesota at that time:

"The people of Minnesota, Mr. President, have stood firmly by you and your administration. They have given both you and it their cordial support. They have not violated any law. They have borne their sufferings with patience, such as few people have ever exhibited under extreme trails. These Indians are now at their mercy; but our people have not risen to slaughter because they believed the President would deal with them justly. We protest against the pardon because if they are not executed the people of Minnesota will dispose of these wretches without law. These two people cannot live together. We do not wish to see mob law inaugurated in

Minnesota, as it certainly will be if you force the people to it. We tremble at the approach of such a condition of things in our state.

"You can give us peace or you can give us lawless violence. We pray you, sir, as in view of all we have suffered, and the danger that still awaits us, let the law be executed. Let justice be done to our people."

Early in December, 1862, while the final decision of the President was delayed, the valley towns of Minnesota, led off by the city of St. Paul, held meetings addressed by the most intelligent speakers of various locations. Among other speakers was United States District Attorney George A. Nouse, of Minnesota, who framed a petition as follows:

"To the President of the United States—We respectfully represent that we have heard with regret the reports of an intention on the part of the United States government to dismiss without punishment the Sioux warriors captured by our soldiers; and further allow the several tribes of Indians lately located upon reservations within the state to remain upon the reservations.

"Against any such policy we respectfully protest in all firmness. The history of this continent presents no event that can compare with the late Sioux massacre outbreak in wanton, unprovoked and fiendish cruelty. All that we have heard of the Indian warfare in the early history of this country is tame in contrast with the atrocities of this late massacre. Without warning, in cold blood, beginning with the murder of their best friends, the whole body of the annuity Sioux Indians commenced a deliberate scheme to exterminate every white person upon the land once occupied by them and by them long ago sold to the United States. In carrying out this bloody scheme they have spared neither age nor sex, only reserving, for the gratification of their brutal lust, the few white women whom the rifle, tomahawk and scalping knife spared. Nor did their fiendish barbarities cease with death, as the mutilated corpses of their victims, disemboweled, cut limb from limb, or chopped into many fragments, will testify. These cruelties, too, were in many cases preceded by a pretense of friendship; and in many instances the victims of more than murderers were shot down in cold blood as soon as their backs were turned, after a cordial shaking of the hand and loud professions of friendship on the part of the murderers.

"We ask that the same judgment should be passed and executed upon these deliberate murderers, these ravishers, these mutilators of their murdered victims, that would be passed upon any white men guilty of the same offense. We ask this not alone for vengeance, but much more as a matter of future safety for our border settlers.

"We further ask that these savages be removed from close proximity to our settlements, to such a distance and such isolation as shall make the people of this state safe from their future attacks."

The final decision of the President, on the 17th of December, 1862, ordering the execution of thirty-nine of the three hundred condemned murderers, disappointed the people of Minnesota. The thirty-nine were to be hung at Mankato on the 26th of December—on Friday.

In pursuance to an act of Congress on the 22nd of April, 1863, and for the purpose of carrying it into execution, the remaining Indians were first taken from the state, on board the steamer "Favorite," carried down the Mississippi, and confined at Davenport, Iowa, where they remained, with only such privileges as are allowed to convicts in the penitentiary. In May, the same year, about two thousand Indians were sent to their reservations in the "land of the Dakotas." Then the 1863 military expedition removed the scattering bands from the borders of Minnesota.

## 29. Facts Concerning the Final Execution

Pictures of the execution of the thirty-eight Indians at Manakto in December, 1862, adorn the shops, public halls and residences of many hundred towns and cities in the great Northwest—almost as well known and often seen as "Custer's Last Fight."

Perhaps no better account of the execution and the crimes for which the Indians executed were charged with can now be obtained than the account narrated by the editor of the *St. Peter Tribune*, he being present. He writes as follows:

Having been ordered to Mankato on business, we were included among witnesses of an execution, the most extensive which has ever been known in the United States, and in punishment of crimes the most atrocious and revolting. Our account must necessarily be brief, and we shall therefore only give such particulars as will prove of interest to our readers and for many of these we are indebted to the *Mankato Record*.

The day was remarkably pleasant for this season of the year, and at early dawn people began to arrive at Mankato on a new and—so far as Minnesota is concerned—unprecedented errand. The streets were already resounding to the tread of the soldiery and citizens, and both were evidently preparing for an event which will always be an important chapter in our history. The great square gallows, standing on the river bluff, showed readiness for the work it was to execute at a later hour of the day. At nine o'clock the military formed a girdle of bayonets around the gallows, and no citizen was permitted inside the enclosure. Captain Burt's company of the Seventh regiment conducted the execution of the following Indians found guilty of crimes charged by the military commission:

1. The-he-hdo-ne-cha (One Who Forbids His House)—Engaged in the massacre; took a white woman prisoner and ravished her.

2. To-zoo, alias Plan-doo-ta (Red Otter).—Convicted of participating in the murder of Mr. Patwell, and of ravishing a young girl.

3. Wy-a-tah-ta-wa (His People). —Confessed to have participated in the murder of Mr. Patwell, and to have taken part in three battles.

4. Hin-han-shoon-ko-yag-ma-ne (Walks Clothed with an Owl's Tail). —Convicted of murder of Alexander Hunter, and having taken and had

Mrs. Hunter as a prisoner until she was rescued from him by another Indian.

5. Ma-za-boon-doo (Iron Blower). —Convicted of the murder of an old man and two children.

6. Wan-pa-do-ta (Red Leaf). —Confessed that he was engaged in the massacre, and that he shot a white man.

7. Wa-he-kna (meaning unknown). —Convicted of murder.

8. Rwa-ma-ne (Tinkling Water). —Convicted of two murders.

9. Rda-in-yan-ka (Rattling Rounder). —Took a prominent part in all the battles, including the attack at New Ulm, leading and urging the Indians forward.

10. Do-wan-za (The Singer). —Convicted of the murder of a white woman, and of the design to ravish her daughter, who was wounded by him and killed by another Indian, before he carried his design into execution.

11. Ha-pan (Second Child). —Confessed that he was in all the battles and at the murder of Mr. Patwell, and that he aided in taking a white woman (Miss Williams) prisoner.

12. Shoon-ka-ska (White Dog). —Was the leader of the party that attacked Captain Marsh's company and was the man who detained Captain Marsh in conversation until the Indians crossed the river and surrounded the command and then gave them the signal to fire.

13. Toon-kan-e-chah-tah-ma-ne (One Who Walks by His Grandfather). —Said in presence of witnesses that he shot a man in an ox wagon, and was in several battles.

14. E-tay-doo-ta (Red Face). —Told witness that he killed Divoll and seven white persons across the river; that the second day after crossing the river he killed a man and a woman.

15. Am-da-cha (Broken to Pieces). —Took witness David Faribault prisoner, who says Am-da-cha shot two persons at his house.

16. Hay-pe-dan (The Third Child). —Cut Mrs. Thieler with a hatchet after she had been shot by another Indian, and fired many shots at the fort.

17. Mah-pe-o-ke-ne-jin (Who Stands on the Cloud). —Convicted of the murder of Antoine Young, and of participating in the murder of a white man and woman.

18. Henry Milord (A half-breed). —Convicted of participating in the murder of a white man and woman.

19. Chas-ka-dan (the First Born if a Son). —Convicted of shooting and cutting a woman who was with child.

20. Baptiste Campbell (A half-breed). —Confessed that he was one of the party who murdered a man and woman, and that he shot first.

21. Ta-tay-ka-gay (Wind Maker). —Convicted of murdering or of participating in the murder of Amos W. Huggins.

22. Ha-pin-kpa (The Tip of the Horn). —Convicted of the murder of Garvie.

23. Hypolite Ange (A half-breed). —Confesses that he was one of the party that murdered a white man, and that he fired at him.

24. No-Pay-Skin (One Who Does Not Flee). —Convicted of participating in the massacre and boasted that he had killed nineteen persons.

25. Wa-kan-tan-ka (Great Spirit). —Convicted of the murder of a white man not named.

26. Toon-kan-ko-yag-ena-gin (One Who Stands Clothed with His Grandfather). —Convicted of participating in the murder of a white man at the Big Woods.

27. Ma-ka-ta-e-ne-jin (One Who Stands on the Earth). —Convicted of participating in the massacre near New Ulm, and encouraging the red men to do so.

28. Paza-koo-tay-wa-ne (One Who Walks Prepared to Shoot). —Convicted of participating in the murder of eight white men.

29. To-tay-hde-dan (Wind Comes Home). —Convicted of participating in the massacre at Beaver Creek, and of taking captive a white woman.

30. Wa-she-choon (Frenchman). —Convicted of the murder of Le Butt's son.

31. Aeche-ga (To Grow Upon). —Convicted of the murder of an old man and two girls.

32. Ho-tan-in-koo (Voice That Appears Coming). —Convicted of the murder of a man at Green Lake, admits that he struck him with an ax after he had been shot by others of the party.

33. Chay-tan-hoon-ka (The Parent Hawk). —Proved to have been one of the party that committed the massacres at Beaver Creek.

34. Chan-ka-hda (Near the Woods). —Is proven to have been one of the party and was present when Patwell was killed, and to have saved Mary Anderson, who had been wounded, from being killed and to have taken her prisoner.

35. O-ya-tay-a-koo (The Coming People). —Convicted of the murder of Patwell.

36. Ma-hoo-way-wa (He Comes for Me). —Convicted of participating in the massacres at Travelers Home and of murdering a man on the road near there.

37. Wa-kin-yan-ne (Little Thunder). —Convicted of participating in the murder, near the Travelers Home, of an old man and two young girls and two boys.

38. Shas-ka

## 30. The Execution

At ten o'clock the prisoners ascended the steps of the gallows, as unconcerned as if they were going to a feast, and after reaching the platform commenced chanting one of their peculiar "he-ahs." Several were smoking, and continued to do so until the rope was cut and they were launched into eternity. One (Shas-ka) manifested his indifference or contempt by exposing his person to the soldiers, and another by throwing his cigar at them and uttering some words which were not understood by those standing near him. The singing was kept up until the platform dropped, and the singular "thug" of the ropes furnished another style of music, and stilled their voices which seemed bold even in the very face of death.

A few showed signs of emotion after the ropes had been adjusted, but a majority hardly noticed this part of the execution. Some even fixed the ropes around their own necks and persistently raised their caps from their faces, until their arms were paralyzed by the fatal plunge.

It was a strange, pitiful sight, but the conduct of the prisoners was enough to remove all feelings of pity in their behalf, and not one of the multitude of spectators expressed regret at the terrible death of these men who had been savages in life and remained apparently defiant or careless to the end.

## 31. The Final Scene

When all was ready, Major Brown, signal officer, beat three distinct taps upon the drum. At the third stroke, William J. Duly, of the mounted scouts (who lost three children during the massacre) cut the rope, the drop fell and thirty-eight savage murderers were launched into eternity.

Some fears had been entertained as to the working of the drop, but it was successful. In a second all but one were suspended by the neck. The rope broke with one, and he fell to the ground, but his neck had been broken in the jerk and fall. He was instantly strung up again. The majority died easily, with scarcely a struggle. A few kicked savagely. We noticed two with clasped hands, remaining in the same position until cut down. Another old man nervously clutched for the hand of the one adjoining, just before the drop fell. As the drop fell, a loud huzza went up from the soldiers and spectators.

Doctors Seignorette and Finch were detailed to examine the bodies, and after all signs of life had disappeared, communicated the death of the prisoners to the officer of the day. The bodies were then taken down.

Four teams were driven to the scaffold. The bodies were deposited in the wagons and an escort conveyed them to the place of burial. Company K, under Captain Burk, without arms, acting as a burial party. The place of burial was the low flat between Front Street and the river, which was overgrown by swamp willows. The burial escort and guard were under command of Lieutenant-Colonel Marshall.

It was generally understood that the prisoners had made a confession to the Rev. Mr. Riggs (the old Presbyterian missionary among the Indians). That gentleman has furnished reports of the conversation with them, but they are simply denials of the charges made at the trial before the military commission. Most of them acknowledged either to have been at the battles or present at some massacre, but said they only used tomahawks on those who had been killed by others, or they shot wide of the mark when compelled to shoot. They all seemed to indorse this sentiment: "Do not think that I killed anyone." But few Indians were present at the execution and not many half-breeds either. Among the number was one Winnebago chief (Baptiste), dressed in white men's clothes. He appeared deeply interested in all the proceedings, and hardly one movement escaped his notice.

We are informed that the Indians who have been executed were very much troubled because many, as guilty as themselves, were left in prison while they were about to die, although the others were equally deserving of punishment.

The police regulations adopted by Colonel Miller were excellent, and the most perfect order was maintained throughout the day; no drunkenness or disorderly conduct was visible in any portion of the town. The military and the citizens seemed to unite in the determination that no disgraceful act should be permitted, but the people themselves gave no cause for its exercise. We do not believe that an equal number of people anywhere could have maintained better order, or given less cause for regret while such a strange scene was being enacted. Only once did the crowd cheer—and that was when the drop fell and the thirty-eight were swinging between heaven and earth.

Thus ends the earthly career of thirty-eight as bold and unflinching malefactors as any nation has ever produced and certainly no equal number approached the gallows with greater courage and more perfect determination to prove how little death can be feared.

# V. Remembrance and Review

## 32. Execution Site

A monument marks the spot of execution and is a reminder to the present passerby of those terrible days of the Sioux massacre in the summer of 1862, when the Civil War was at its height, and the government had all it could possibly do to survive as a nation.

Of the thirty-eight Indians who were executed, thirty-three were converted to the Catholic faith, through the efforts of two priests of rare ability and true spiritual advisers. The other five who were executed were converted to the Protestant faith under Missionary Williams, of the Presbyterian church. The colonel in command at the execution gave both Protestant and Catholic clergymen all possible chance to be with the prisoners during the last few days before their execution.

## 33. Indian Massacre Monument

The beautiful and impressive monument seen on the hill near the court house square at New Ulm, was erected by the state of Minnesota, in 1890, to commemorate the battle with the Sioux Indians in August, 1862. It is an imitation of real bronze. The Legislature appointed the following as a committee to plan and erect this monument: Gen. Henry H. Sibley, Hon. John F. Meagher, of Mankato; Dr. Asa W. Daniels, of St. Peter, and Col. William Pfaender, of New Ulm. The monument is twenty-seven feet high and stands on a base seven feet square. It is at the junction of Center and State streets and overlooks the scene of bloodshed between the savages and whites. It bears numerous inscriptions, among which is this: "This monument is erected by the State of Minnesota to commemorate the battles and incidents of the Sioux Indian War of 1862, which particularly relates to the town of New Ulm.—1890."

Another inscription gives the roster of those who were killed in this awful siege at New Ulm, and is substantially as follows:

"Eleventh Regiment State Militia.—G. W. Otto Barth, Jacob Castor, William England, Julius Kirschstein, Matthias Meyer, August Roepke, Leopold Senzke.

"LeSueur Tigers No. 1.—Fifth Sergeant William Maloney, Matthew Aherin, Washington Kulp.

"The Mankato Company.—Newell E. Houghton, William Nicholson

"St. Peter Frontier Guards.—First Lieutenant William B. Dodd, Max Haack, Jerry Quane, Luke Smith, John Summers, Rufus Huggins.

"New Ulm Company.—Ferdinand Krause, August Reimans.

"Milford Company.—Jacob Haeberle.

"Citizens killed on August 19, 1862, returning from a reconnaissance.—A. D. Loomis, Uri Loomis, William Tuttle, William Carroll, George Lamb, DeWitt Lemon, Ole Olson, Jan Tormon."

The monument was unveiled by Dr. A. W. Daniels, of St. Peter, who had served as a surgeon during the siege. At the same time several salutes were fired by the battery of the town. The chief oration on the occasion of the dedication of this monument was made by Hon. John F. Meagher, of

Mankato, and was responded to by Governor Merriam in well-chosen language.

The only thing to mar the beauty and appropriation of this shaft is the fact that the medallion of some worthy citizen of New Ulm who bravely fought during that massacre period, was not placed beside that of Judge Charles Flandrau, who with others came to the rescue with soldiers.

## 34. The Milford Tablet

In the month of September, 1914, a "marker" or memorial tablet was dedicated by the Junior Pioneers Society in commemoration of the Milford Massacre. On Sunday afternoon the monument was finally dedicated, although the work had been commenced two years prior to that date. Hon. Albert Pfaender and Capt. Albert Steinhauser made the principal addresses—one in German and one in English. Several hundred people had assembled from New Ulm, Milford Township, Springfield, Morgan, Sleepy Eye and other points to take part in the ceremonies. After the speeches had been offered there was a picnic held in Anton Henle's "Palm Garden" near by the site of the monument. Capt. Albert Steinhauser, as president of the Junior Pioneers Society, delivered an address in the German language, which was well received. Athanasius Henle acted as chairman of the day. At the close of Captain Steinhauser's address he delivered the deed to the property upon which stand the tablet and monument, over to the township board of Milford Township. Louis Spelbrink, chairman of the board, in response thanked the Junior Pioneers for the monument and assured the organization that every effort would be made to keep the monument and grounds in proper condition.

Hon. Albert Pfaender made an eloquent address in the English language which was published in the *Brown County Journal*, and of which the subjoined are extracts:

"It will avail nothing to dwell on the horrors of that great massacre. The cruelty with which the savages treated their victims was in many cases shocking in the extreme. There were some instances of hair-breath and almost miraculous escapes from the hands of the bloodthirsty invaders.

"Suffice it to say that all told fifty-four persons were killed by the savages in the immediate neighborhood—those whose names are inscribed on this monument. It is undoubtedly true that had it not been for the settlement of Milford and the warning given by the presence of the Indians here, the city of New Ulm would have been utterly surprised by the redskins and the place easily taken by them. On the other hand it was perhaps New Ulm that prevented the entire population of Milford Township from being killed.

"It is sad to contemplate that which seems to be established now; that the wrath of the Indians was aroused by wrongful acts of the whites themselves, and being unjustly treated the savage instinct of the Sioux asserted itself and urged them to those terrible deeds of violence. If it is true that the unscrupulous agents of the government and those in league with them, willfully defrauded the trustful Indians, then they even in their vaunted state of civilization, were more guilty than the simple savages, for their acts of perfidy only brought to life an inborn lust to kill and destroy, which once aroused knows no bounds."

## 35. The Monument.

This memorial tablet consists of a solid concrete shaft six feet high, by three feet square at the base and tapering to its top. At the bottom of this block the soil is near to that where flowed the innocent blood of the massacred. A large bronze tablet, attached to and imbedded into the cement work, bears the impressive inscriptions. This tablet faces the public highway and contains the names of the fifty-three who were killed by the Indians. A part of the inscription reads as follows:

"This tablet was erected by the Junior Pioneers in memory of the following men, women, and children of the township of Milford who were massacred by the Indians during the Indian outbreak in 1862."

Then follow the names, and it is the ardent wish of the pioneers and their children and children's children, that the names be here printed in the permanent annals of this county, that generations yet unborn may read of their untimely deaths:

John Martin Fink, Monika Fink, his wife; Max Fink, his son; Carl Merkle, his grandson. Florian Hartman. John Baptiste Zettel, Barbara Zettel, his wife; Elizabeth Zettel, their daughter. Max Zeller, Lucretia, his wife; John, their son; Monika, their daughter; Cecilia, their daughter, Conrad and Martin, their sons. Anton Messmer, Mary Ann, his wife; Joseph, their son. Martin, Anton and Mary Henkle, children of Anton Henkle. Frank Massapust, Mary Ann, his wife; Mary and Julia, their children; Frank, their grandson. John Rohner, Barbara, his wife, and one child. Sebastian May, Barbara, his wife; Henry and Bertha, their children. Henry Heyers, Dorothea Heyers, his wife; Carl, John and Joachim, their sons. Mrs. Joseph Stocker. Benedict Drezler, Frank, his son. Christ Haag, Adolph Schilling, John Keck, Mrs. Brigitta Pelzel, Fred Guth, Joseph Emmerich. George Roessr, Barbara, his wife. Theresia Eggensdoefer."

## 36. As Viewed by Bishop Whipple

Bishop Whipple, that great and spotless character of the Episcopal church in Minnesota, wrote concerning the crimes and causes connected with the massacre as follows:

"There is not a man in America, who ever gave an hour's reflection to the subject, who does not know that our Indian system is an organized system of robbery and has been for years a disgrace to the nation. It has left savage men without governmental control; it has looked on unconcerned at every crime against the laws of God and man; it has fostered savage life by wasting thousands of dollars in the purchase of tomahawks, paint, beads and scalping knives; it has fostered a system of trade which robbed the thrifty and virtuous to pay the debts of the indolent and vicious; it has squandered the funds for civilization and schools and has connived at theft; it has winked at murder, and at last, after dragging the savage down to a brutishness unknown to his fathers, it has brought a harvest of blood to our own door."

## 37. Pensioners of the Sioux Uprising

About 1902 the state of Minnesota passed an act by which all defenders at the time of the Indian massacre who were in any way injured or became afflicted by bodily ailment as a result of that war, subsequently, should receive a pension, which was fixed at twelve dollars per month. In many instances this small pension from the state has materially aided those who fought for their homes and families in 1862.

# VI. Appendix

## 38. Establishment of Ft. Ridgely

Ft. Ridgely was a noted United States military post, in Ridgely township. Nicollet County, established by the government in 1853 as a protection for the frontier against the Indians. With the establishment of the lower Indian Agency in the summer of 1853 the establishing of this post became a necessity. The concentration of so many bands of Indians upon so small an area rendered the situation important and worthy of attention. A military post was necessary to preserve order among the savages and remind them that the "Great Father" was keeping watch over them, ready to protect and encourage the good and to repress and punish the bad. There were to be two Indian agencies on the reservation. The Upper Agency for the Sissetons and Wahpatons, established at the mouth of the Yellow Medicine and the Lower Agency, for the Medawanton and Wahpekoota bands, was placed at about six miles east of the mouth of Redwood River. Both agencies were on the south bank of the Minnesota River.

The matter of a new military post was called to the attention of C. M. Conrad, then secretary of war, and Gen. Winfield Scott, commander of the regular army, by delegate Henry M. Sibley. General Scott concurred in Sibley's recommendations, the secretary of war approved it and issued necessary orders. In the autumn of 1852, Capt Napoleon Jackson Tecumseh Dana, of the quartermaster's department and Col. Thomas Lee, then in command at Ft. Snelling, were ordered to select a site for the new fort—"on the St. Peter River (now Minnesota) above the mouth of the Blue Earth."

In the latter part of November, with an escort of dragoons from Ft. Snelling, and after a three days' march in the snow, the officers reached La Framboise's trading post at the Little rock. Five miles above the rock on the crest of the high bluffs, on the south side of the Minnesota River the site was fixed. The new post was named "Ridgely" in honor of Maj. Randolph Ridgely, a gallant officer of the regular army from Maryland, who died of injuries received at the battle of Monterery, Mexico. When Ft. Ridgely was established, Ft. Riley, Kansas, was ordered built. At the same time, Ft. Dodge, Iowa, and Ft. Scott, Kansas, were ordered discontinued and broken up. Ft. Ridgely took the place of Ft. Dodge and Ft. Riley was substituted for Ft. Scott.

The first garrison at Ft. Ridgely was composed of Company C and K went up on the steamboat "West Newton" from Ft. Snelling, but later were joined by Company E which marched across the country from Ft. Dodge, Iowa, and arrived on June 11, 1853, when work on the buildings was begun. When Company E arrived, its captain, Brevet-Major Samuel Woods, previously well identified with Minnesota history, took command, by virtue of his rank. The work of construction was in charge of Captain Dana.

This fort was a noted post during the Indian outbreak of 1862. Since 1868 the fort has not been occupied and the buildings have been allowed to go to utter decay. It was closely connected with the Indian wars of Minnesota and Dakota. All that remains of any interest now is the cemetery in which are situated two monuments—one to the honor of Captain Marsh and the brave men of his command; the other dedicated to Mrs. Dr. Eliza Mueller, who devoted herself to the care of the wounded at the time of the Sioux outbreak. A railroad was once projected from the south, known as the Ft. Dodge & Ft. Ridgely, which was to pass through this section, but a survey turned its course to that of the present Minneapolis & St. Louis.

## 39. Siege of the Fort.

[By Charles S. Brant, author of the well-known work entitled, *History of the Minnesota Valley*, from which is taken the following, perhaps the most authentic account of this siege.]

Foiled on the attack of New Ulm by the timely arrival of reinforcements under Colonel Flandrau, the Indians turned their attention toward Ft. Ridgely, eighteen miles northwest. On Wednesday, at about one o'clock in the afternoon, August 20, the attack commenced. It was not unexpected, however, as some authors put it, for the garrison had pickets out for several days and at no time within ___ days could Indians have "surprised" the soldiers there.

The fort is situated on the edge of the prairie about half mile from the Minnesota River, a timbered bottom intervening and a wooded ravine running up out of the bottom around two sides of the fort within about twenty ___ of the buildings, affording shelter for an enemy on three sides.

The first knowledge of the garrison had of the presence of the foe was given by a volley from the ravine which drove in the pickets. The men were instantly formed by order of Lieutenant Sheehan in line of battle on the parade ground inside the works. Two men, Mark M. Grear, of Company C, and William Goode, of Company B, fell at the first fire of the concealed foe after the line of battle was formed—the former was instantly killed, the latter badly wounded, both being shot in the head. Robert Baker, a citizen who had escaped from the massacre at the Lower Agency, was shot through the head and instantly killed while standing at a window in the barracks at about the same time. The men soon broke for shelter and from behind boxes, from windows, from the shelter of the buildings and from every spot where concealment was possible, watched their opportunities, wasted no ammunition, but poured their shot with deadly effect upon the wily and savage foe, whenever he suffered himself to be seen.

The forces in the fort at this time were the remnant of Company B, Fifth Regiment, Lieutenant Culver, fifty-one men: about fifty men of Company C, same regiment, Lieutenant Sheehan; the Renville Rangers, Lieutenant Gorman, numbering fifty men—all under command of Lieutenant Sheehan. There were also about twenty-five armed citizens. Sgt. John Jones, of the regular army, a brave and skillful man, was stationed at this fort as post sergeant, in charge of the ordnance, and took immediate command of the artillery, of which there were in the fort six pieces. Three only, however, were used—two six-pound howitzers and one twenty-four pounder field-piece. A sufficient number of men had been detailed to work these guns and at the instant of the first alarm, were promptly at their post. One of the guns was placed in charge of a citizen named J. C. Whipple, an old artillerist, who had seen service in the Mexican War and in the United States Navy, and had made his escape from the massacre at the Lower Agency; and one in charge of Sergeant McGrew, of Company C. The other in charge of Sergeant Jones in person. In this assault there were probably not less than five hundred warriors led by their renowned chief, Little Crow.

So sudden had been the outbreak and so weak was the garrison that there had been no time to construct any defense work whatever, or to remove or destroy the wooden structures and hay stacks in which the enemy could take position and shelter. The magazines were situated some twenty rods outside the main works on the open prairie. Men were at once detailed to take the ammunition into the fort. Theirs was the post of danger—but they passed through the leaden storm unscathed.

In the rear of the barracks was a ravine up which the St. Peter road passed. The enemy had possession of this ravine and road, while others were posted in the buildings at the windows and in sheltered portions in the sheds in the rear of the office quarters. Here they fought from three o'clock until dark, the artillery all the while shelling the ravine at short range and the rifles and muskets of the men dropping the yelling demons like autumn leaves. In the meantime the Indians had got into some of the old out-buildings and had crawled up behind the hay stacks from which they poured a heavy volley into the fort. A few well-directed shells from the howitzers set them on fire and when night rolled over the scene the lurid light of the burning buildings shot up with a frightful glare and served the purpose of revealing to the weary sentinel the lurking foe should he again appear.

The Indians retired with the closing day and were soon in large numbers on their ponies, making their way rapidly toward the agency. The great danger feared by all was that under cover of darkness the savages might creep up to the buildings and with fire-arrows ignite the dry roofs of the wooden structures. But about midnight the heavens opened and the earth was deluged with rain, effectually preventing the consummation of such a design, if it was intended. As the first great drops fell upon the upturned faces, there was a glad shout of "Rain, rain, thank God." Stout-hearted, strong-armed men breathed free again; and the weary, frightened women and children slept once more in comparative safety.

In this engagement there were two men killed and nine wounded and the government mules were stampeded by the Indians. Jack Frazir, an old resident of the Indian country, volunteered as bearer of dispatches to Governor Ramsey, and availing himself of the darkness and the furious storm made his way safely out of the fort and reached St. Peter where he met Colonel Sibley and his command on their way to the relief of the fort.

Rain continued to fall until nearly night Thursday when it ceased and the stars looked down upon the weary but still wakeful and vigilant watchers in Ft. Ridgely. On that night a large quantity of oats in sacks, stored in the granary, near the stables, and a quantity of cord-wood piled near the fort, were disposed about the works in such a manner as to afford protection for the men in case of another attack. The roof of the commissary building was covered with earth, as a protection against fire-arrows. The water in the fort had given out, and as there was neither well nor cistern in the works, the garrison were depend upon spring, some sixty rods distant in the ravine, for a supply of that indispensable element. The only recourse was now to dig for water, which they did at another, less-exposed point, and by noon had a supply sufficient for two or three days, secured inside the fort.

### THE ATTACK RENEWED

In the meantime the small arms ammunition having become nearly exhausted in the battle of Wednesday, the balls were removed from some of the spherical case-shots and a party of men and women made them into cartridges which were greatly needed. Small parties of the Indians had been seen about the fort, out of range, during Thursday and Friday forenoons, watching the fort to report reinforcements had reached it.

At about one o'clock in the afternoon Friday, the $22^{nd}$ they appeared again in force, their numbers greatly augmented, and commenced a furious and most determined assault. They came apparently from the Lower

Agency, passing down the Minnesota bottoms and around into the ravine surrounding the fort. As they passed by the beautiful residence of R. H. Randall, post sutler, they applied the torch and it was soon wrapped in flames. On came the painted savages yelling like demons let loose from the bottomless pit; but the brave men in that sore-pressed garrison, knowing full well that to be taken alive was certain death to themselves and all within the fort, each man was promptly at his post.

The main attack was directed against that side of the works next to the river, the buildings here being frame structures, and the most vulnerable part of the fort. This side was covered by the stables, granary and one of the old buildings, besides the sutler's store on the west side. Made bold by their augmented numbers and the non-arrival of reinforcements to the garrison, the Indians pressed on, seemingly determined to rush at once into the works, but were met, as they reached the end of the timber and swept round up the ravine, with such a deadly volley of musketry poured upon them from behind barracks and the windows of the quarters, and of grape and canister and shell from the guns of the heroic Jones, Whipple and McGrew, that they beat a hasty retreat to the friendly shelter of the bottom, out of musket range. But the shells continued to scream wildly through the air, and burst around and among them. They soon rallied and took possession of the stable and other outbuildings on the south side of the fort, from which they poured terrific volleys upon the frail side of the wooden buildings, the bullets actually passing through their sides, and through the partitions inside of them. Here Joseph Vanosse, a citizen, was shot through the body by a ball which came through the side of the building. They were soon driven from the buildings by the artillery, which shelled them out, setting the buildings on fire. The scene now became grand and terrific. The flames and smoke of the burning buildings, the wild demoniac yells of the savage besiegers, the roaring of canon, the screaming of the shells as they hurled through the air, the sharp crack of the rifle, and the unceasing rattle of musketry, presented an exhibition never to be forgotten by those who witnessed it.

The Indians retired hastily from the burning buildings, the men in the fort sending a shower of bullets among them as they disappeared over the bluffs toward the bottoms. With wild yells they now circled round into the ravine, and from the tall grass, lying on their faces, and from the shelter of the timber, continued the battle till night, their leader, Little Crow, vainly ordering them to charge on the guns. They formed once for that purpose, about sundown, but a shell and round of canister sent into their midst closed the contest, when with an unearthly yell of rage and disappointment, they left. These shots, as was afterward learned, killed and wounded seventeen of their number. Jones continued to shell the ravine and timber round the fort until after dark when the firing ceased, and then, as had been done on the night before, since the investment of the fort, the men all went to their several posts to wait and watch for the coming of the wily foe. The night waned slowly; but they must not sleep; their foe is sleepless, and that wide area of dry shingled roof must be closely scanned and the approaches be vigilantly guarded, by which he may under cover of darkness, creep upon them unawares.

Morning broke at last, the sun rose up in a clear, cloudless sky, but foe came not. The day passed away, and no attack; the night again, then another day; and yet other days and nights of weary, sleepless watching but neither friend or foe approached the fort until about daylight on Wednesday morning, the 27th, when the cry was heard from the lookout on the roof, "There are horsemen coming on the St. Peter road across the ravine." Are they friends or foes, was the question on the tongues of all. By their cautious movements they were evidently reconnoitering and it was yet too dark for those in the fort to be able to tell at that distance friend from foe. But as daylight advanced, one hundred and fifty mounted men were seen dashing through the ravine; and amid the wild hurrahs of the assembled garrison, Col. Samuel McPhail at the head of two companies of citizen cavalry, rode into the fort. In command of a company of these men were Anson Northrup, from Minneapolis, an old frontiersman, and R. H. Chittendon, of the First Wisconsin Cavalry. This force had ridden all night having left St. Peter, forty-five miles distant, at six o'clock the night before. From them the garrison learned that heavy reinforcements were on their way to their relief under Col. (Later brigadier-general) H. H. Sibley. The worn out and exhausted garrison could now sleep with a feeling of security. The number of killed and wounded of the enemy is not known but must have been considerable, as at the close of the battle they were seen carrying away their dead and wounded. Our own fallen heroes were buried on the edge of the prairie near the fort and the injuries of the wounded men were carefully attended to by the skillful and excellent post surgeon, Dr Alfred Mueller.

## Tribute to Mrs. Eliza Mueller

We close our account of the protracted siege by a slight tribute on behalf of the sick and wounded in that garrison to one whose name will ever be mentioned by them with love and respect. The hospitals of Sebastopol had their Florence Nightingale and over every blood-stained field of the south in our own struggle for national life, hovered the angels of mercy, cheering and soothing the sick and wounded, smoothing the pillows and closing the eyes of our fallen braves. And when in after years the brave men who fell sorely wounded in the battles of Ft. Ridgely, Birch Coulie and Wood Lake, fighting against the savage hordes who overran the borders of our beautiful state in August and September, 1862, carrying the flaming torch, the gleaming tomahawk and bloody scalping knife to hundreds of peaceful homes, shall tell their children and children's children the story of the "dark and bloody ground," of Minnesota and shall exhibit to them the scars those wounds have left, they will tell with moistened cheek and swelling hearts of the noble, womanly deeds of Mrs. Eliza Mueller, the "Florence Nightingale" of Ft. Ridgely.

## Sergeant John Jones

We feel that the truth of history will not be fully vindicated should we fail to bestow upon a brave and gallant officer that need of praise so justly due him. The only officer of experience left in the fort by the death of its brave commandant was Sergeant John Jones, of the regular army artillery; and it is but just to that gallant officer that we should say but for his cool courage and discretion, Ft. Ridgely would in the first day's battle have become a funeral pyre for all within its walls. And it gives us more than ordinary pleasure to record the fact that the services he here rendered in defense of the frontier were fully recognized and rewarded with a commission of captain of the Second Minnesota Battery

## Recollections of O. G. Wall

[O. G. Wall, who was then in his teens, and who participated in the expeditions against the Indians as a member of Captain Marsh's company, and saw service with General Sibley in 1863, kept a daily diary of all passing events of importance during all those trying days on the frontier.

Twenty years later, having entirely forgotten that upon leaving for the far West to engage in business he gave his mother his diary, while back home on a visit his mother handed him the book and he utilized those previous entries in the publication known as "Recollections of the Sioux Massacre." From this work are taken several extracts.]

At about ten o'clock in the forenoon, August 18, 1862, came like lightening flash from a clear sky, the startling news of the horrible massacre begun three hours previously at the Redwood Agency. Down from the northwest, nearing the fort, was seen the approach of people in great haste. The attention of the garrison was generally attracted to the unusual spectacle, but without once suspecting the cause of it. J. C. Dickinson was in advance and was the first to enter the fort. He had scarcely told in a few words of the uprising when a team immediately followed him and entered under lash with a load of refugees, among them a wounded man, who had made his escape after being wounded at the Lower Agency. That savage wrath had burst like a flame was at first inconceivable, but the testimony that the scalping-knife had flashed from its sheath to follow the deadly work of the gun was all too evident to be questioned. The soldiers gathered around the refugees, whose tales were told in a shocking manner and in dramatic detail. Captain Marsh, commander of Ft. Ridgely, did not deliberate, but ordered the assembling of the company at once. Charles M. Culver, the drummer-boy, for the first time sounded with meaning emphasis the long-roll. Thrilled with the story of the massacre and the clamor of the drum, men were quickly in line to receive orders. With a haste that seemed imperative a detail of forty-six men was made at once to proceed to the scene of carnage, under the belief that the situation was yet controllable, and in any event demanded the presence of soldiery at the Lower Agency. It was simply a matter of moments between the receipt of the news and the departure of Captain Marsh and his detail for the scene of the bloody work thirteen miles away.

At the command "Forward," the men moved out with elastic step, the very embodiment of splendid soldiery. Teams were hastily hitched up, and carrying light supplies of ammunition and provisions, followed and soon overtook the command. Captain Marsh and interpreter Quinn were on mule-back, and the men now climbed into the wagons that the better time might be made in reaching the agency.

Ft. Ridgely was now practically deserted, Lt. T. P. Gere remaining in command of the post with less than thirty men.

## CAPTAIN MARSH PLANS TO RESTORE ORDER

Fugitives who came in over the Agency road, and had met Captain Marsh and his men, pronounced the expedition to the ferry one destined to end in the greatest disaster. This was neither reassuring nor comforting to the remnant of the company left in the fort, and was rendered less so because the convictions expressed were those of men of keen discernment, who were well informed on the deplorable situation. In fact, these fugitives, when meeting Captain Marsh, cautioned him of his danger, and advised him if he would not turn back, at least not to enter the valley of the Minnesota River, which he must do three miles from the Lower Agency if he persisted in reaching the ferry.

Before Captain Marsh had covered half the distance to the agency his command had witnessed buildings aflame and corpses by the wayside to warn him of the danger that threatened him, and whole frontier as well. There was no time to deliberate. To march into the jaws of death, as seemed imminent, might make the fall of Ft. Ridgely a certainty, and thus expose the frontier settlement to annihilation. On the other hand, if a brave and almost superhuman effort could yet stay the savage hand dripping with blood, incalculable loss of life could be prevented. Captain Marsh knew his men. He had no doubt of their splendid courage. The fleeing refugees warned them that to enter the valley was almost certain death, but all this was met with a stoical determination to do faithfully and bravely the duty pointed out to them by their commander, who believed the great good possible to be accomplished was worth the hazard the undertaking involved.

While this march was being made on the quiet summer day, hearts were beating anxiously at the fort. As the men passed out to the northwestward in the forenoon, they watched for a mile or so, and disappeared, with a "bon voyage," below the intervening prairie ridge, entering as it proved, on the threshold of eternity. Refugees came in increasing numbers, and pointed to the distant columns of smoke as those of burning homes. Some of these people were wounded and all were fatigued and terror-stricken.

There were none so dull as not to realize that the situation was profoundly critical. Marsh and his little detail were well within the environment of the savages. That they would stay the bloody hand, or even extricate themselves from their perilous predicament, became hourly more doubtful. There was no reserve force to go to their assistance. The fort itself and all in it must fall if vigorously attacked. This was self-evident.

When within six miles of the agency Captain Marsh, seeing evidences of danger on every hand, ordered his men to abandon the wagons and resume their former order of march. The pace of the men was quickened, and believing the Lower Agency the center of the disturbance, and that once their cool, wise heads could be conferred with and a stop put to the hellish work, the command hurried with a zeal worthy of a better fate than awaited the brave detachment. Reaching the top of Faribault hill, three miles from the agency, a view of the Minnesota Valley presented itself. Sickening scenes had been witnessed by the wayside, and there was little else than desolation to be seen from the hilltop. Only men of the rarest courage and of the most perfect discipline would have entered that valley of death in the face of all that was known.

### AMBUSH PLANNED BY THE INDIANS

At the fort the horrible condition of the Lower Agency had now been fully detailed, striking terror in every heart and sealing the doom of Marsh and his men. Among the refugees who arrived in the afternoon from the agency was Rev. J. D. Hinman, an Episcopal missionary, stationed at Redwood. He had started between six and seven o'clock that morning from the agency to make a trip to Faribault, when unusual signs for that hour in the day among the Indians attracted his attention. The Indians were almost naked, and carried their guns. Their numbers increased, and the people began to wonder at their unusual appearance, which some interpreted to mean that a raid was to be made on some Chippewa band known to have invaded the neighborhood. The Indians squatted on the steps of various buildings, their demeanor betraying no sign of hostility.

Now a signal gun broke the silence in the upper part of town. Even this was doubted to be a sign of hostility until other shooting up the street and hasty fleeing of the people toward the bluffs overlooking the river became alarming. White Dog ran past Mr. Hinman at this juncture, and to an inquiring word replied that "awful work had been started." He was no doubt himself taken by surprise, though later in the day his cunning and his treachery played an important part in the betrayal of Marsh. Little Crow also passed Hinman about this time, but with a scowl declined to answer an inquiry of the missionary, through they knew each other well, and the chief now sullen, had always been polite and friendly. The firing had now become a fusillade, and the people were being shot down on every hand. The traders were the first objects of hatred to fall, riddled with bullets. As the bloody work progressed the savages grew wild and furious, their hideous yells, the crash of their guns, work of the torch, the shrieks of their helpless victims, begging vainly for mercy, creating a scene horrifying in the extreme. Reverend Hinman fled before the spreading tide of death and had reached the river, fortunately found a skiff with which he hastily crossed, making good his escape to Ft. Ridgely.

Private James Dunn and William B. Hutchinson were the first to arrive at the fort with the story of the frightful disaster at the ferry, they having been dispatched by Sgt. John F. Bishop, who was in command of the only known remnant of Company B to escape the merciless slaughter at the ferry. The little party were carrying a badly wounded comrade, while Bishop himself was wounded. Their progress being thus impeded, Bishop dispatched Dunn and Hutchinson to apprize the garrison of the disaster, himself and party reaching the fort at ten o'clock at night.

### THE STRUGGLE AT THE FERRY

Captain Marsh's slender detachment descended the Minnesota valley at Faribault hill at about mid-day and marched across the bottom for three miles over a road not unfavorable to a treacherous foe, grass of a rank growth affording them shelter on either hand. When within a mile or so of the ferry (as Privates Dunn and Hutchinson relate the story), the captain halted his men for a moment's needed rest. Resuming his march the men were moved in open order by single file to minimize the danger from exposure, and in this order continued to the ferry-house, situated on the east side of the road, ten or twelve rods north from the ferry.

Along the river, at the ferry, were clumps of willows and other brush, together with a rank growth of weeds and grass, with here and there a sandbar deposited by the river in flood-time. Knowing the stealthy nature of the Sioux, and that war had been inaugurated, the surroundings were such as any American soldier, willing to meet his foe in the open, would feel ill at ease in.

On the high bluff just across the river was the Redwood agency, the objective point of Captain Marsh, and where he had hoped to meet prominent Sioux chiefs, and through their co-operation restore order. He apparently could not realize that the agency had been blotted out, and that every soul that had made up its white citizenship lay prostrate where he fell, shot to death and mutilated beyond recognition. The slope leading from the river to the brow of the agency hill was studded with a thick growth of bushy timber. The disemboweled body of the ferryman had already been found, with the ferry boat on the north side of the river, ready for the soldiers to enter upon, as the Indians had no doubt carefully planned, divining that Marsh would seek to cross to the agency side.

Indians there were in plenty concealed, but kept very quiet. A few warriors on horseback revealed themselves indifferently on the prairie south of the agency, and at a considerable distance from the ferry, their evident purpose being to attract attention from the forces masked in the region of the ferry. Near the ferry landing on the opposite side of the river from the agency, was a lone Indian, chosen for a conspicuous part in the tragedy to be enacted when the plans of the cunning Indians were matured. This was recognized to be no less personage than White Dog, who himself was clearly taken by surprise by the outbreak, as his demeanor to Reverend Hinman revealed in the early morning. White Dog was a prominent Indian at the agency, having been president of the Indian Farmers Organization and his selection as a man likely to inspire confidence in Captain Marsh was neither spontaneous nor accidental. Through interpreter Quinn, Captain Marsh addressed White Dog, who in reply, suavely invited Marsh across the river, assuring him that the Indians did not wish to fight the soldiers, and that if Marsh would cross to the agency a council would be called to meet and confer with him. Two soldiers who went to the river's brink to obtain water as this conversation was being carried on, discovered in concealment on the opposite side, near White Dog, many Indians. However, Captain Marsh ordered his men forward from the ferry house to the ferry landing, purposing to cross, his men halting at a front along the river. Sergeant Bishop having stepped to the water's edge for a drink as the ferry ropes were being adjusted, saw evidences in the roily condition of the water that Indians were crossing up-stream with a view of a rear attack. This conviction expressed to Captain Marsh, was intuitively grasped by White Dog, who knew the moment was critical, and now doubted that Marsh would enter the ferry. He therefore fired the signal gun, as was his part in the tragedy, to which Quinn, the white-haired interpreter, sensing its meaning instantly, in his last breath cried, "Look out!" A deadly volley came from the ambuscade on the opposite side of the river, killing many a brave soldier who had no opportunity to defend himself. Quinn was among those to fall at the first volley, riddled with no less than a dozen bullets. The volley was high and mainly passed over the soldiers' heads. Marsh and Quinn stood nearly side by side when the volley was fired, but the Captain was unscathed, and instantly ordered his men to fall back to the ferry house. Now came the awful realization of Bishop's prediction, for with deafening yells there rose from ambush in the rear, and within short range, a legion of naked frantic devils who poured a merciless volley into the already staggered ranks of Marsh. The effect was deadly. Now the men fought for their lives, and to extricate themselves from their perilous predicament. The losses were already so great that to attempt a stand would be simply to blindly challenge fate. As stated by Chaska in 1863, when referring to this bloody incident, White Dog gave the death-signal prematurely, for which he was bitterly assailed by Little Crow and other prominent leaders in the massacre. The signal was not to have been given until the savage cordon had been so extended as to prevent the escape of a single man of Marsh's command, in the event the soldiers could not be gotten upon the ferry and there annihilated.

## DEATH OF CAPTAIN MARSH

By this time the Indians had secured possession of the ferry house. The fighting now was of the most desperate character, being hand to hand, or a few paces range. The soldiers made deadly work among the ranks of the savages, who were no match for the trained infantrymen in open combat; but realizing they could not withstand the already overwhelming and constantly increasing numbers, Marsh gave the order to gain at all hazards the thicket along the river, of which the savages had not yet secured possession. This was accomplished under a furious fire, fifteen out of the original number, after fighting like demons, reaching the sheltering copse.

To reach the fort over an unknown country, pathless, and beset with a desperate enemy, was the only hope of the brave commander and his shattered forces. The thicket was raked with guns of the savages, but the men were now fighting from cover with a deliberateness of aim that kept the enemy well at bay. Covering their retreat carefully, the men fought their way down through the brush until they apparently must soon expose themselves to Indians seen out on the fort road, who were believed to be moving eastward to intercept the retreating detachment. Captain Marsh believed that safety lay alone in crossing to the south bank of the river, and led in an effort to accomplish this end. This was about four o'clock p.m. At this point the Minnesota River was fifty or more yards across. Lifting his sword and revolver above his head the Captain waded successfully two-thirds of the way across. Getting beyond his depth he could no longer retain his weapons of defense, and dropping them, attempted to swim. In this he was unsuccessful, and called to his men for assistance. Brennan, Dunn and Van Buren, all men of heroic mold, hastened to the rescue of their commander, but he was doomed by the treacherous waters and though seized by the strong arm of Brennan as he was sinking the second time and brought to the surface, and although the Captain grasped the shoulder of the athletic hero daring all to save him, the hold of the officer and that of the soldier were broken in the struggle, and Captain Marsh disappeared beneath the merciless waters to rise no more.

Now the command devolved upon Sgt. John F. Bishops, than whom there was no better or braver soldier. Beset with calamity, dogged with disaster and wounded besides, with one of his men, Private Svendson, so seriously wounded that he must be carried by his comrades, Bishop was put to test summoning all his tact, courage and endurance. He at once decided to keep the north side of the river and not attempt its crossing as had Marsh. This decided the fate of the little company now left. There were only fourteen men and Sergeant Bishop. The Indians, believing they had crossed the river, also crossed and lay in ambush for them. While the mistaken Sioux were lying there awaiting the soldiers made their escape under cover of hills to a safer place. Night came on and Ft. Ridgely several miles in the distance, and in fact they half believed that the Indians had destroyed the post. But Bishop sent Privates Dunn and Hutchinson, as before related on into the fort, and twelve hours from the time the company under Marsh had left the garrison what there were left of them arrived at the garrison.

In that eventful day there were lost, including Captain Marsh, who was drowned, twenty-five men and five wounded, but who recovered.

### EXPERIENCE OF SUTHERLAND

Early on the morning of August 20, William A. Sutherland and William Blodgett arrived at the fort, after experiences and endurances almost unbelievable. These men were shot down in the engagement at the ferry. Their escape, their sufferings and their heroic struggle for life can scarcely be matched in history. Sutherland was shot in the breast, the ball passing through the right lung and out near the point of the shoulder blade, at his back.

The wound rendered him unconscious for a time, and while in this condition the Indians took from him his gun, cartridge-belt and box, his cap, coat and shoes leaving him destitute of clothing, save his shirt and trousers. The mystery is that he was not scalped, but his escape was no doubt due to a distracted state among the savages, who were rent with dissension over the personal effects of their victims. Sutherland fell near the river, where he lay for several hours. Returning to consciousness, he found himself crazed with pain and thirst. Lifting his head cautiously, he looked about him, half stupefied, yet curious to learn whether his comrades, who were in action when he fell, had been annihilated. While the savages had completed their hellish work, they were still in the vicinity, and he heard their voices near, and the firing of guns far and near warned him of havoc being wrought upon the settlement. He determined to crawl to the river to slake his thirst, even though to do so should cost him his life. He tested his strength in an effort to turn over, having fallen on his face when shot. He found he could move his body, and down through the high grass and weeds he dragged himself to the water's edge, leaving a trail stained with blood to betray him should an Indian cross his path. He was much refreshed with copious droughts of water and crawled back into the weeds, where he meditated and wondered if escape was possible for him. He reasoned that no attempt to escape should be made until nightfall. Thirst compelled him to make several trips to the river. Near his drinking place was a skiff lodged against the river's bank, and partly filled with water. The water-logged boat suggested a possible means of escape and he resolved that if not discovered and slain before dark he would make a superhuman effort to save his life. At about ten o'clock at night, after all the savages had joined in the hideous orgies of the scalp-dance on the agency side of the river, he felt that now if ever he must carry out his resolution. He crept cautiously to the water's edge, removed as much water from the boat as possible with his hands while the craft lay on its edge, then pushed it into the stream, and got in. There was no seat in the boat, no oars or paddles, and nothing with which to bail out the water of which there was considerable at the outset. He sat down in this in the bottom of the boat, hatless and without clothing to protect his shattered body from the penetrating chill of night, with no nourishment of any kind. Thus he began his silent journey, dependent wholly upon his boat and the current of the sluggish river. As he drifted silently away under the southwestern hills, the hideous din of the scalp-dance, conducted but a matter rods away from where he had lain for hours, became less and less distinct, until croaking frogs or an occasional bittern alone broke the silence of night. In this helpless plight, this country boy of twenty summers, who had left all the comforts of a happy home, tenanted with loved ones, to enter the army and serve his country, began a voyage, under conditions seeming to challenge fate and which fiction, in all its reckless extravagance, would scarce attempt to parallel.

All that night, all the next day, and all the following night, until nearly dawn, this ghostly figure drifted silently along, now backwards, now sidewise and now for an hour or so whirled helplessly in an eddy. The nights were gloomy and solemn, but not more so than the light of day, that revealed the pall of death on every hand. Sutherland was seized with delusions that haunted him against reason, from the outset of his journey. He felt that he was helplessly being carried in the wrong direction—that he should go up stream instead of down, and this fantasy gave him no end of trouble. He was shot on Monday afternoon. He entered his boat Monday night, and there remained until the break of day Wednesday morning. He knew his progress had been very slow, but he felt that if the boat had carried him in the proper direction, he must be in the vicinity of the fort. At all events he found that he must abandon the waterlogged boat, for he had become so stiffened he would scarcely move. Against his better judgment, the bewildering delusion that had been his pursuing nemesis, impelled him to land, by paddling with his hands on the wrong side of the river, or on the side opposite the fort. Benumbed and weakened, but stimulated with the hope that he would soon reach the garrison, he picked his way through a jungle of underbrush, and out of the valley and up the wooded hills until he reached the open prairie on the highlands. He saw Indian cabins that were strange to him, but no trace of the garrison or of any familiar object. His heart sickened, despair overwhelmed him and he sank to the earth. But his great will power triumphed, and he rose to his feet again.

The sun had now risen to flood the earth with its exhilarating light. Sutherland realized that he must return to the shelter of the river valley, as he was in great danger of being discovered; and as he turned his face to the northward and west, to his amazing astonishment and joy he beheld Ft. Ridgely in the favoring light of the morning sun, on the hills beyond the river, the colors flying at full mast, assuring him that without doubt the fort had not fallen. He now knew that he abandoned his boat not far above the road crossing the river by the ferry, and leading to the fort. He set out to reach the river at the ferry crossing, but on his arrival at the stream a new disappointment awaited him. The rope spanning the river had been cut and the ferry was gone. There was but one alternative; he must swim the river or perish in the attempt to do so. He lost no time, but got down into the water, which was soon beyond his depth, compelling him, while suffering excruciating pain in the effort, to exert himself to keep from sinking. By the assistance of the current he landed on the opposite side, where having been carried several rods down stream, he experienced great difficulty in pulling himself up the abrupt and brush-grown river bank. He accomplished all this, however, and walked a mile, most of the way up hill, and reached the fort, a gaunt, bent, bloodstained, half-naked specter, as if risen from the dead to affright his surviving comrades. He arrived in the garrison between eight and nine o'clock, Wednesday morning, August 20, and an hour later the Indians came in swarms over the road by which he had barely made his escape. Sutherland recovered and served with his company in the south until the close of the Civil War.

## 40. Indian History and Treaties

When Spain ceded the territory now including Minnesota to the United States, it was subject, of course, to all the former rights of the Indian tribes found herein. It was left to the United States to subdue, or drive away the Indians, or better still to make treaties and purchase the lands from them, as they might from time to time be needed. this latter was carried out in a large degree, along legitimate lines and in a business way which, at least, was satisfactory to the tribes at the date of making such treaties.

The treaty that mostly interests the citizens of Brown county, was that made at Traverse des Sioux in July, 1851, with the Sioux tribes. This ceded to the white man all the Sioux Indians holdings except a strip of ten miles in width along either side of the Minnesota River. This tract of now very valuable land, running from New Ulm to Lake Traverse, would have been held by the Indians had they not made war against the whites in 1862, by doing this they lost all title to such lands and were driven from the state of Minnesota, as a tribe. Hence, this was the first and last treaty with the Indians in this state that has had to do with the people of Brown county.

### INDIAN CHARACTERS

The Dakota or Sioux Indians were divided into four great tribes: Medawakonton, Wahpekuta, Wahpeton and Sisseston, who held a large territory west of the Mississippi; from the borders of Iowa along the Mississippi, up to the Minnesota, and stretching far into Dakota. They had great bodily strength, a slim and pleasing stature, and were remarkable for their shrewdness and deceit. Their features are rather long, and they have a dark, though not repulsive complexion. The subjoined account was written of them long years before they had caused the pioneers of the Northwest so much trouble in their warfare:

"They are continually wandering about and consequently use for means of subsistence whatever Nature affords them. Fishing and hunting are their principal sources of support. In the spring of the year they often make sugar and syrup from the juice of the maple, and during the summer they gather wild rice and berries. This work is done by the squaws. The Indian regards his wife as a slave, and he thinks it below his dignity to do hard work. When they travel, the women not only carry the papooses and baggage, but also lead the beasts of burden, which in the absence of a wagon or sled, carry the tepee upon their backs. He often compels her, although weighed down under a heavy burden, to carry even his gun so that he can trot along with greater ease. When they find a place where fuel and water are convenient, or where hunting and fishing are good, the women will have to go to work and set up the tepees and bring in whatever is necessary, except the game, which he provides. A few so-called civilized Indians till the soil, but they seldom raise anything except corn and potatoes. These dress like the whites, and they were formerly supplied by the government with farming implements, horses, cattle, etc. They are very proud of their dress, which consists merely of a high hat and a shirt. These Indians are usually despised by the real Indians who treat every kind of a head dress with a contempt, except their own peculiar one, and whose only covering consists of a woolen blanket or a buffalo robe; and they live in tents or tepees. These prefer to dress gaily, cover themselves with all manner of trumpetry, and fold the skin of an animal around their body so as to look as much as possible like the animal itself.

"In summer months they appear mostly in garb of the old original Adam, with the addition of a gun and a smoking pipe. Their arms are bows and arrows, guns, knives, and a sort of hatchet called a tomahawk. Their necessaries of life are few and very simple. They never wash their meat, and seem to have a dislike for water except "firewater" (whiskey). Still they very much like a clean white shirt. A kettle, a few pots and the skins of animals compose all their furniture, and they eat their food, especially their meats, half raw, and devour even the entrails raw. Their appetite is prodigious. Whenever they obtain anything palatable they eat and eat without regard to their real needs or the coming day. Hence it not unfrequently happens that they are compelled to fast for days at a time. They are not much troubled with any disease, except the small-pox, and their medicine-men have in vain tried by all manner of sorceries and strange appliances to banish that dreaded complaint. A cripple, lame or deaf and dumb, is seldom found. They love their ponies, and keep as many as possible. But during the winter they lose a great many because they are too lazy to provide hay for them. With no barns and little food they die off before spring comes. They believe in a Great Spirit Manitou, think much of ceremonies over their dead, but hang them up on posts to be exposed to the elements until they are dried up. Their romantic life, their fidelity, their friendship and strength of character, which some writers tell us about, is pleasant sentimental reading—that's all.

"The Indian is always serious, seldom laughs or jokes, and is an uncomfortable and mistrustful companion. He understands begging above all things. He never forgets an offense, but is quite apt to forget acts of kindness. With the Indian revenge is a virtue and they practice polygamy. Their hospitality, however, is worthy of all praise. The stranger receives the best pelts for his bed, and the host keeps up a warm fire with his own hands if the pale-face happens to remain in his tent over night during the winter. They are skillful in the use of arms, keen in the chase and relentless in pursuing an enemy; they love noisy musical instruments and dance after their own peculiar fashion. Their natural senses are sharp and more fully developed than those of the whites. They are very cruel in war, and prefer deceit and stratagem to an open battle. After a fight they scalp their dead enemies before they think of carrying off the booty; for they take great pride in possessing a large number of scalps, because this indicates the number of enemies slain by them. They ornament their heads with feathers, which they consider "wakan" (holy). They can endure more hardships than the white race and are wonderful runners, many of them being able to overtake a swift horse. In hiding their feelings and in self-control they can do wonders. They suffer pain with stolid indifference, and their wounds heal quickly. To leave one of their dead in the hands of the enemy is looked upon as a foreboding evil and the greatest ignominy that could possibly happen to them."

## Seven Weeks' Captivity of Benedict Juni

Benedict Juni is still a resident of New Ulm. His own story of his capture by the Indians when only eleven years of age, is a testimony that there were some kind Indians and that the milk of human kindness was exhibited for nearly two months to a mere lad, and that during the awful outbreak in Minnesota in the summer of 1862. At that date his father was on a farm between Beaver Falls and Morton, five miles north of the Lower Agency. The story is as follows:

On August 18, 1862, while seated at the breakfast table, a noise so unusual that it caused comment, was at intervals heard by us in the direction of the Lower Agency. My father said it was the beating of drums announcing the arrival of soldiers. In reality it was the first volleys fired by the Indians at the defenseless whites. The previous day having been a Sunday, our working oxen had been left out at large. I mounted our only horse and brought them in. My father was just hitching up a wagon when our nearest neighbors, John and Mike Hayden, and the latter's wife, approached our place in great haste and told us that the Indians were on the warpath. My father was disinclined to take it seriously, but yielding to the pleadings of the women, took the hayrack off and replaced the box, hurriedly threw in some clothing, bedding and provisions, and put the women and children in also. A Mr. Zimmerman and his eldest son took charge of the wagon. They had two guns and an old sword with which Mr. Zimmerman declared he would defend the occupants. On the way down the valley he picked up the rest of the family, consisting of his wife and two sons and two daughters.

### Attacked by Redskins

His progress was unobstructed until he reached Faribault's place, where he and two of his sons were killed before they had a chance to make any use of their weapons. The women and children were imprisoned in the house, and the Indians had a hot debate about what to do with them. Some wanted to set the house on fire, but finally milder counsel prevailed and the women and children were allowed to pursue their way to Ft. Ridgely on foot.

My father, about the time the women and children started off from our place in the wagon with Zimmermans, ordered me to round up our milch cows and young stock and take them to a place now occupied by the village of Morton. I was then to proceed down the valley to alarm the settlers, while he and my younger brother guarded the herd. But I was not fated to call on many settlers that morning. The Indians interfered with our program. First they came upon my father, who was guarding the cattle, and drove him off into the open prairie. Their guns were significant and he took their advice to decamp, reaching Ft. Ridgely before any of the rest of the family.

### WARNS NEIGHBORS

Meanwhile I had taken the path laid out for me. I called at two places, Mr. Bureau's and Mr. Kumrows. Both families had already been told of the danger and were making ready to escape. They asked me to go with them but I declined, as that would have interfered with carrying out my instructions. My road led me through a gap in the high rocks. I had gotten within a hundred yards of this spot when I saw three Indians coming out of the pass. I obligingly turned my horse, intending to go around the bluff and avoid meeting them. But almost immediately three guns were leveled on me, and just as obligingly I came to a halt, having a high regard for the Redman's marksmanship.

### DEPRIVED OF HIS HORSE

One of the Indians now took the horse by the bit and asked me if I intended to resist. I answered only with a smile at the thought of an unarmed boy only eleven years old resisting three armed men. At that he turned the horse around and started in the direction I had come. The thought struck me that perhaps he thought more of the horse than he did of me, so I slipped off. He swung himself on and trotted away without deigning to notice me further. His companions seemingly well pleased with the performance followed their leader. I was free again. Thus far I had known no fear at all. But I thought it prudent to give the road a wide berth by going around the bluff rather than through it. Before again reaching the road I saw the first dead lying in the grass. It was the body of a Frenchman, one of two brothers who were operating the ferry at which Captain Marsh and his command were annihilated a few hours later.

### DOG GUARDS DEAD MASTER

I can never forget the appealing look the murdered man's little dog gave me as he sat beside his master licking the clotted blood from his face. Thenceforth my movements were guided by more caution. Indians, wagons and oxen, among them our own, passed me while I lay in the grass a few rods away. Whenever the Indians had disappeared I would run until I saw new signs of danger, when I would hide again. In this manner I reached Faribault's place about noon.

I saw a group of Indians outside the house, the same group as I afterwards learned, which was deciding the fate of my people. One look was enough. I dashed into the cornfield on the opposite side of the road and made a detour around the usual fording place and thus missed seeing what happened at Faribault's place.

On the east side of the stream the road left the valley and wound up the hill toward Manager's place. The underbrush now impeded my progress and I again ventured into the road. When half way up the hill I was suddenly confronted with two young warriors who came round a sharp turn. One carried a double barreled shotgun and the other a bow. The one with the bow got ready instantly to send an arrow through me, but his companion quickly thrust the bow aside with the butt of his gun.

### Captured by Foemen

"Where go?" he asked me. I answered that I was bound for "Tepee tauke," or "Big House" as the Indians called the fort. He shook his head to indicate that I was mistaken, and ordered me to face about and precede them down the hill. This was the beginning of my seven weeks' captivity.

The trip down the hill to the ford occupied but a few minutes. Here we came suddenly on evidences of the brutal work of the Indians that day. The body of John Zimmerman lay by the stream. It was stretched as naturally as though it was taking a noonday nap. This was what I thought until I tried to rouse him. Then I discovered that John would wake no more. The body of his brother Gottfried lay in the water, he having been shot while trying to escape on a log. The father of the boys lay on the west side of the stream. My captors must have suspected that he was still living, for they rolled him over and crushed his skull with blows from the butt of the gun. Scattered about were a few household goods that had been thrown on the wagon at home. I picked up some article of clothing, but was ordered to drop it. A couple of books were there. We had only two at our house, Webster's speller and the Bible. I tucked the latter under my arm, but was compelled to drop that, too.

### Whipped by Captors

It appeared that my captors had been on a reconnoitering expedition toward the fort and were in a hurry to get back and report. The party in the house, including my mother, one brother and two sisters, must have gone before this, for all was quiet in and about the place. The Indians all had vanished. My captors and I started on again. I had my trousers rolled up and one of the Indians having a blacksnake whip, gave me an occasional cut across the bare calves. The object was two-fold. It afforded him great amusement to see me jump and it considerably accelerated my speed.

On arriving at the ferry I noticed a great congestion of traffic. Four of five wagons drawn by oxen were awaiting transfer. There was great confusion. The Indians had managed pretty well so far, but coaxing the oxen onto the ferry was another matter. I stepped up to the foremost team and soon it followed me onto the boat. This act brought hand-clappings and calls of "Hocksheta washtav" (good boy).

It was not long till all had passed to the south or agency side of the river. Here I was allowed to rest a quarter of an hour or more. Seated on the high bank, I watched the gun practice of the Indians, who had many new guns taken from the stores, and some taken from their victims but a few hours before, and with which they wanted to get acquainted before Captain Marsh and his men should arrive on the scene. You would never guess the target. They were moving targets. Stacks of milk pans had been taken from the stores. Each marksman took one and hurled it with a spinning motion out into the stream, allowed it to right itself and float some distance with the current, and taking good aim, fired. There was no need of a scorer. The bright pan would tell the story. The conditions in the battle fought some hours later were quite similar. It was an easy change from floating pans to the heads of swimming soldiers.

## MENACED BY DRUNKEN RED

One of my captors remained at the ferry to be on hand when the enemy appeared. The others took me up the hill to the agency. Here some of the buildings were burned, others were just plundered. I saw the Indians carry a man out of one. Whether he was dead or alive I could not tell. Some of the Indians had taken too much fire-water and were turned into demons. One brandished a butcher knife, made a lunge at me, but a thrust from the butt of the gun of my captor and protector sent him reeling. It was my third escape from death in the day and perhaps the closest. When nearing the edge of the agency, an Indian drove by with my father's wagon and oxen. Delighted at seeing something from home, I exclaimed, "Oh, there is our team."

My captor replied, "Well, if it is ours, let's take a ride." He hailed the driver who took us on. I immediately assumed control of the team of oxen.

### UNWILLING AID OF INDIANS

On arriving at an Indian village my captor left me at the hut of his future mother-in-law, a widow with two grown daughters. Here several squaws were squatted around an open fire on the ground. They had bags of shot which they poured into a ladle and then melted over the fire and poured into bullet molds. There was a heap of bullets on the ground, with the nipple made by the hole in the mold still on them. One of the squaws ordered me to get busy with a knife cutting off these projecting nipples. The bullets were then placed in the empty shot bags and sent to the ferry by Indian lads. Thus I became unwillingly an instrument in killing some of Captain Marsh's men.

Like most boys, I had great faith in the prowess of soldiers and believed them invincible if pitted against Indians. Repeatedly I told the squaws that they would "get their pay," meaning their punishment, for what they had done, but conveying no meaning thus, so that if they showed displeasure I could explain that I meant their annual payment from the government.

### WHEN HOPE ALMOST DIED

About four o'clock in the afternoon a flag came in view in the direction of the agency. Soon after was seen the glitter of bayonets and swords. What I had firmly believed all day was now to come true. The soldiers were coming to mete out punishment and release the captives. I could contain myself no longer, and having no hat I picked up an old rag, clambered on the roof of an old hut, waved it and shouted several lusty hurrahs. Then I jumped down and ran toward the procession. Alas, the approaching parade was a mob of wild Indians arrayed in the garb of soldiers they had slain at the ferry. This disillusionment was the worst shock of the day for me. I then and there gave up all hope of seeing white people again. Had not the invincible soldiers been annihilated?

### Dressed as Indian

On the second or third day of my captivity several squaws assisted my mistress in making a regular Indian outfit for me. It consisted of a pair of leggings, a calico shirt, a breechcloth and a belt. In dress I was now like an Indian, but my complexion was fair and my hair silvery white. This naturally made me conspicuous in a group of Indian boys and I was soon known all over the camp as "Paw Skaw" (whitehead). At first I did not mind it, but it finally affected my temper to a point where the squaw demanded to know what was the matter. I told her. She found a remedy. Thereafter when she had mopped my face with a wet rag as she did every morning, she scattered dried powder over my head, smeared my face with paint, made a few streaks and dots in it with her finger nails. This worked like a charm and I was no longer annoyed.

### Changes Employers

The Indian who had captured our teams and wagon remembered how well the oxen had obeyed me. He soon found me again and asked me to help him haul some forage. Having accompanied him two or three times, the squaw, on my last return, said to me that if I worked for others I must board and lodge there, too. The next time my Indian friend came I told him what the squaw had said. "So much the better," he replied, "come right along. Hereafter you are a member of my family."

In my new home, I found a trunk that had belonged to an uncle of mine who was a soldier in the federal army in the South. In it I found a few copies of *Harper's Weekly* with pictures, mostly war scenes, and these interested me much. My master had two sons and one daughter. The eldest boy was of my age and proved to be a good companion and true friend to me. Nor was I entirely forgotten by the family that had first sheltered me.

### Well Liked by Captors

The two daughters called one afternoon and got permission to take me back with them for a day. Every attention was paid me. I was feasted and entertained with pleasant chat by the two girls.

For fear I may be considered a pampered drone in the hive I ought to make mention of the duties I was expected to perform. I had to provide all the wood and water for the cooking, whether the supply was far or near. I had to see to the feeding of the oxen and horses. I had to assist in pitching camp, loading and unloading and when on the move had charge of the ox-team.

The food of the Indians was good. Our rations were liberal. Green corn, potatoes and beans, fresh mutton or beef were the staple articles. Vegetables and meats were served without salt and the coffee was black and very sweet. I protested a little and to please me a little bag of sugar and salt was put to my place and I was told to use both to suit my taste. Sometimes when strolling through the camp after a meal I would be invited to partake and never refused. One time it was the white porcelain dishes and at another the regular plantation molasses that attracted me.

### Regarded as a Prodigy

Sometimes when visitors came I was the subject of conversation. I had learned to read but not to use a pen, but my master would point to me as a prodigy who could read and write. I was able to understand and answer questions about ordinary affairs. But at times I was asked questions by my Indian captors and their friends touching astronomy and religion which were, of course, beyond my depth.

At the time the battle of Birch Coulee was raging there was great excitement in the camp. My mistress feared for my safety. Toward evening she took me into the woods skirting the bluffs south of the Minnesota River, placed me in a hollow basswood tree and told me to remain until she came the next morning. The position was cramped and uncomfortable and when it was dark I crept out and ran home to camp where I went to sleep in my usual place. On seeing me the next morning she was greatly surprised, but did not seem displeased. There were disturbances at other times when my master was at home. On these occasions he was accustomed to roll me in a buffalo robe and sit on me, calmly smoking until the danger, whatever it was, was over.

On the night that the Indians lay around General Sibley's camp at Wood Lake, I slept in the powder tent on a heap of powder, which made a better mattress than one would suppose. I slept soundly.

## Surrendered to Soldiers

On his return from the Wood Lake battle, my master told me to get ready to return to my parents, as arrangements had been made for a surrender. On the next morning I put on my white man's garb, such as could be found. It consisted of a pair of man's trousers with the legs cut off at the knee, a long linen duster and a stove-pipe hat.

In this garb I was surrendered to the soldiers, and confined in a sort of enclosure with other surrendered prisoners whose names were taken and sent to the *Pioneer* at St. Paul. In this way my father came to learn that his boy was still in the land of the living. But the end of my adventures had not yet come. Two other boys and myself—Louis Kitzmann and August Gluth—being tired of this confinement, escaped from the white soldiers, and I was captured again by the Indians and again surrendered when some of the Indians decided to quit the warpath and come in. My companions got away entirely and reached Ft. Ridgely before I did. In the camp of the Indians I waited upon women and messed with three little girls. One tin dish and one tin spoon constituted our outfit and rice and sugar the only food except some wormy crackers. My two companions, Kitzmann and Gluth, left Camp Release on the first opportunity and reached Ft. Ridgely on the same day that my father and Mr. Gluth had come to look for us. Kitzmann's father was not there. He had been killed at the outbreak of the massacre. My experiences at the fort were not of the most pleasing character. I now realized fully that to be a captive among the Sioux was not the worst lot that could have befallen me. Within a few days of my arrival at the fort my father took me to LeSueur where I had a home until the autumn of 1865.

## 41. Pioneer Settlement

In many countries the tracing out of the first settlers, establishing who were the first actual settlers, where they located and how long they remained, is a hard task to successfully accomplish by the local historian, but here in Brown County and New Ulm, such is not the case, as there has been left a permanent record of all such first and important events, and it is a pleasure to enter at once upon this work, drawing from such records and published accounts as are at hand, both in this county and at the rooms of the Minnesota Historical Society, at St. Paul. the author is further aided by the few persons who still linger this side the strand, and whose memory goes back and they easily bring to notice the events of the fifties, when Brown County had its first white settlers.

### THE FIRST SETTLER

Prior to 1853, the year before the government surveyed the lands in what is now Brown County, there were no white men, but the green solitude of the flower-covered prairies and beautiful wooded glens and valleys were all held by the Indian, whose rights up to then had never been disputed by his pale-faced brother. To Edward McCole, who came across from Nicollet County in 1853, must be ascribed the honor of being Brown County's first settler. His cabin was burned and while he was away his claim was jumped by Anton Kaus; this claim later comprised the farm owned by Colonel Pfaender.

### COLONIZATION SOCIETIES

The next settlement was affected by the Chicago Land Verein, who came in the autumn of 1854. This was one of two colonization societies, each having similar designs. These were the "Chicago Land Verein" and the "Colonization Society of North America," the latter having its origin in the city of Cincinnati, Ohio. Eventually a union of the two took place, as will presently be observed. The result was the formation of the "German Land Association."

The Chicago Land Verein was organized in Chicago in the summer of 1853, by a class of six Germans who were studying the language of their adopted country. Among the six persons was Frederick Beinhorn, who conceived the idea of a colonization society. The notion met with favor and public meetings were held and an organization was perfected, of which Frederick Beinhorn was president, Frederick Metzke was secretary, and a Mr. Schwarz, treasurer. The teacher of this class was William Fach, who was appointed to look up a location for the association, the object of which was to get beyond the reach of greedy land speculators, to obtain government land and create a model town, which should be surrounded by gardens. One of the necessary conditions also, of the intended site of the city, was that the site should face a river frontage. By November of the first year the society numbered sixty-three; meetings were held every week, and a monthly fee of ten cents was required from each member, to defray necessary expenses. In February, 1854, the society gave a ball at the old market house on the north side, in Chicago, which affair netted them three hundred dollars. Notice was given through the papers that a fee of three dollars would thereafter be required for the enrollment of any new members, if joining before eight days from publication of such notice. After then five dollars would be exacted. It was not long before the membership had swelled to eight hundred persons, nearly all of whom were working men. The agent then informed them that he had selected a tract of land in every way suitable to the needs of the proposed colony. This was in April 1854. Investigation, however, proved that such lands were situated in a sandy desert-like region in the northern portion of Michigan.

A committee, consisting of Beinhorn, Assal, Hummelscheim, Mueller and (Voehringer) was then appointed to select an eligible site for settlement, according to the expressed desire of the society. After visiting many places, principally in Iowa, they returned to Chicago without finding what they wanted. Soon afterward, Pfeiffer and Messerschmidt were sent to Minnesota, and reported good land in the neighborhood of Swan Lake. Members Kiessling and Weiss were sent out to corroborate this good news, and upon their return reported they had found a very good place on the opposite side of the Minnesota River from a place called "LeSueur." This was in September, 1854. An expedition of twenty members was fitted out to go to the place selected. Upon their arrival they were not well pleased, and proceeded up the river to Traverse des Sioux. Athanasius Henle, Ludwig Meyer, Frederick Massapust and Alois Palmer started for Ft. Ridgely, and arrived at the trading post of Joseph LaFramboise (a Canadian Frenchman), who said there was a place near the Cottonwood where it flowed into the Minnesota River, that was the most eligible place in the entire state for a town.

Arriving on a site of the present city of New Ulm they were charmed with the situation, and sent for their companions, who had remained at Traverse des Sioux, who arrived October 8. These hardy men made their way into the wilds of Minnesota, from Chicago to Galena, fifteen miles by rail, thence by steamer to St. Paul. The distance from their future home was about six hundred miles. Henle, Massapust and Walser had set out on their journey ahead of the others, and when they reached Stillwater they were sorely tempted to remain there.

At St. Paul, the little company, except Henle, Walser and Haeberle, went aboard the "Jeanette Roberts" and sailed to Ft. Snelling, six miles above St. Paul, thence up the Minnesota River toward their destination. The three men named above preferred to go by team, the distance from St. Paul being only seventy miles. Having reached Henderson the party put up for the night, intending to go to LeSueur the next day, as it was only four miles. LeSueur then contained only three or four houses, but the party was met by a band of about four hundred Indians in war costume and savage appearance. About that time they had the misfortune to have their wagon overturn, whereupon the warriors turned out and assisted the party to get righted up again. The fear they had felt before was now all gone. The remainder of the colony arrived at LeSueur by steamer, and from thence they went together to see the much-talked-of-land on the west side of the Minnesota River. It was three miles from the village of LeSueur, on the left bank of the stream, on a plateau steeply from the water's edge. That was the chosen townsite that had been picked out for them. No one was pleased over it. True, there was an extensive forest at hand and plenty of water in the river. There was also a beautiful meadow at the foot of the hill through which a canal could be dug as had been discussed on the journey from Chicago. Still this site was rejected. The townsite did not offer them even a drink of water and the September day was very hot and they uncommonly thirsty. The well-matured plans of a canal, a zig-zag street, etc., were all abandoned and they bid the place a lingering farewell, and returned to LeSueur, from which place the next day they went to Traverse des Sioux, a place they had heard much of, and only fourteen miles distant. At Traverse they met a man who had much to say about a fine townsite and induced eleven of the party the following day to go and look at it. It was about eight miles from Traverse. They found tall slough grass all about it. No one except the townsite shark was favorably impressed with the site, and he did all the talking. He spoke of the placid waters of Swan Lake being lead to the Minnesota by the construction of a canal and of how great factories and breweries might be propelled from its waters.

## JOSEPH LA FRAMBOISE, TRADER

Seven of the party returned to Traverse des Sioux. The remaining four—A. Henle, Ludwig Meyer, Fr. Massapust and Alois Palmer—wanted to prospect the district west from Swan Lake which appeared extremely inviting from a distance, and, at all hazards, find a place better than the ones already looked upon. After having spent a chilly night amid the high prairie grass, they simply wandered along the shores of the lake in a westerly direction. Hunger and fatigue came upon them, they found a trail on which a company of soldiers were just then marching toward the newly erected Ft. Ridgely. They met a German soldier who took pity on his countrymen and gave them a small piece of bacon and a potato of unusual size. Being refreshed, they continued their journey on west and at dusk their steps were directed to a shanty, but found it vacant. It belonged to a half-breed who had deserted the hut and gone to the Sioux agency on business. But they kept steadily pressing onward and at last came upon the house of Joseph La Framboise, a French-Canadian trader who had married a squaw. The party were well feasted there on the flesh of muskrats and strong black coffee. This place was four miles from Ft. Ridgely and thirty-four from Traverse des Sioux. Through this noble old pioneer trader the party were induced to look at the present site of the city of New Ulm. After a long, tedious march with but little to eat or drink, they trudged along until they found two deserted Indian huts, made of long poles about two inches in diameter, set up in the form of a circle, and covered with bark. Tired and hungry they stretched their weary limbs out for a night's rest. When they awoke in the early morning, the sun high heavenward, they observed that they were in the midst of a real Indian village, but that the same was then deserted. They also noted a number of corpses hoisted upon eight foot poles, a mode of burial with some of the tribes. Bleaching bones and grinning skulls were not the most inviting sight. But the beauty of the natural scenery—the Cottonwood and Minnesota valleys—worked like magic on their tired brains. They all, with one accord, agreed that this was the place they had long been seeking—a suitable townsite and adjoining farming section. They walked back to Traverse des Sioux the same day, and upon their arrival about midnight, found most of their companions still up and they asked if they had found a good location. The prospectors replied, "We have found a very fine place; the houses are already to move into and the graveyard is close at hand." They had referenced to the Indian huts and the corpses they had seen on the poles. The company finally went to bed, but were early risers and heard the wonderful story of the new-found land. This was on October 8, 1854. The entire party set out from Traverse des Sioux and soon found their new home, and without an exception they all agreed that the site was ideal.

In this connection it should be said that the company now numbered about thirty men, principally made up of immigrants from Europe who, on account of cholera in Chicago, desired to go west, and were neither acquainted with the hardships of frontier life in general nor with the rigor of a Minnesota climate. But they were constituted of the right make-up and were eventually crowned with signal success.

### First Immigrants Named

Among the first party of immigrants who arrived at the newly chosen spot were: M. Wall, Walser, the two Henle brothers, Dambach, the two brothers Haeberle, Ludwig Meyer, W. Winklemann, Palmer, Kleinknecht, the two Mack brothers, L. Hermann and wife, Kraemer, Schwartz, Weiss, Elise Finke, afterward married to A. Henle; Julius, with wife and child; Thiele, Boeringen, Wiedmann, Massapust; Zettel, with wife and child, J. Brandt, Kock and Drexler. Many of these daring men and women were massacred in the Sioux outbreak in the summer and autumn of 1862.

From some of the men who braved those early-day hardships it has been learned that they provided for winter quarters the first winter about as follows: An Indian had already informed the party that it were better for them to move away from there. Remembering now that the district where the prospectors had found hospitality and good quarters with the trader La Framboise was well covered with heavy timber and shrubbery, and that he was friendly to them, furthermore that they would be near the fort in case of need, they resolved to spend the winter in that neighborhood. They broke camp and went up the Minnesota River, crossing their future townsite. Four miles from La Framboise's they found an Indian village. The Indians having gone to the fort for their annuity they took possession of their huts until they could finish a small log cabin for themselves. Provisions soon began to dwindle away, two barrels of flour and the few potatoes they had bought of a half-breed, only lasted about two weeks. The dangers of the situation were not at first understood by the colony. The nearest places from which food could possibly be had was Ft. Ridgely, ten miles above them and Traverse des Sioux, thirty-five miles to the east. They had only one wagon and four oxen, two of which soon died, and the remaining two were very poor and too weak to draw an empty wagon. They had very little hay. They had some gold coin, but had it not been for the good trader, La Framboise, they must have certainly starved, and as it was they suffered much from hunger at times during that first winter.

The Mack brothers finally undertook a trip to Ft. Ridgely for supplies and lost their bearing and finally came up at an Indian camp, where they were feasted and kept all night and put on the right tract. On the way back the next day they were belated and had to lodge beneath a tree the following night. About this time another thoughtful member, Joseph Dambach, undertook a trip to St. Paul for provisions. They were then happy in the thought that the Indians would not return till spring and they could occupy their quarters at the Indian village mentioned before. At Ft. Ridgely they could not always get supplies—they ran races at times to see who should get the refuse materials thrown out, such as hog heads, cattle heads, etc. Sometimes two or three would start out in the dead of the night to outdo others who had intended to go. Fortunate, indeed, was he who could offer a few drinks of whisky to the soldiers, by which act he could obtain more and better provisions from the government stores. A saw-mill near the fort was a place for exchange and barter with the soldiers and settlers. It was there many a drink of whisky was exchanged for vegetables and other things the settlers were in need of.

The Indians, however, came back and claimed the use of their huts in the dead of winter, and it was only through La Framboise and his influence that the red men set up other quarters for that season nearer La Framboise. During the winter the small-pox broke out among the Indians and they left the place altogether. The tepees of the neighboring village had been deprived of their coverings, hides and robes. One corpse was left behind. This was doubtless a superstition of the Sioux who made it a practice to leave one body in honor of the Great Spirit. They never came to claim the body and after the wolves had nearly devoured it the settlers buried the remainder of it.

Fortunately, that was a mild winter, compared to many in Minnesota. The Indians frequently returned and traded with the settlers and asked for food, which they always got, but they did not exact the Indian's homemade trinkets in return. Thus they came and went on friendly terms and many a Sioux who was the recipient of favors at the hands of the settlers at that time returned the same during the fatal month of August, 1862, with his deadly tomahawk and bullet.

### Settlers Burned Out

By February the snow had gotten very deep. They had cleared away a site for a saw-mill to be erected in the coming spring. They had plenty of fuel and a fair supply of provision by this time. On the fifteenth of that memorable month, which was a very cold day, they built on uncommonly large fire in the three stoves they had, and one of the stovepipes set fire to the straw and bark roof. The fire was not seen until the whole cabin was on fire. The burning cinders dropped on the floor and on the bedding on which one of the party was lying sick. the cabin, and with it many of the necessities of life, burned, but no one was injured. After this they were obliged to enter the miserable huts left by the Indians as worthless. Provisions were again getting low and but little could be had at the fort. La Framboise had given them some straw with which they covered one of their huts and put stove in it. But this was poor protection against the severe cold northwest winds and frosts. Their victuals froze on their plates while they tried to eat a meal. During that winter the Henle's and Zettel cut the lumber for their buildings with their own hands.

Spring finally came and was welcome to all the members of the colony, who had suffered as no pen can describe. Now the matter of fixing exactly where the permanent townsite should be exercised the minds of the colony—some favored one place and some another. It was designed by some to utilize the waters of the swift-flowing Cottonwood for milling and factory purposes, hence this faction desired that the town be built near that spot. But the survey went forward and the place chosen was the present city of New Ulm, the most of which was burned in the August, 1862, Indian massacre period, but soon rose from the embers and ashes to be a well-built, modern city. A greater part of the city as known today is made from additions made to the original tract platted. The first houses were built in 1855 by Adam Behnke, A. Dederich, Ludwig Ensderle, Paul Hitz, Ludwig Meyer, H. Meierding and C. Staus.

The first settlers were largely Swabians, and in remembrance of the city of Ulm they named their town "New Ulm."

## MORE ARRIVALS

On May 16, 1855, about twenty more members of this society arrived from Chicago, among them one Volk, who according to instructions from the president laid out the townsite of New Ulm. On May 20, the same season, a branch of the home society was established, of which A. Kiessling was elected president; John Zettel, vice-president; Henry Meyerding, secretary and Joseph Dambach, treasurer, their terms of office being for three months. It was about this date when the president in Chicago, F. Beinhorn, decided that every member of the society should pay into the treasury the sum of thirty dollars, so as to enable the land to be purchased. This was responded to by two hundred and fifty men paying in the sum called for. When the money was thus paid in, the treasurer, Albert Blatz, brother of Valentine Blatz, the famous brewer of Milwaukee, and the president, Beinhorn, set out for New Ulm, May 10, 1856, with funds with which to purchase the land of the government. Upon arrival it was found that in order to claim land under the preemption laws, more houses must be erected, and as soon as this could be done, Beinhorn and Blatz, in company with Charles E. Flandrau and fourteen claimants, went to the land office at Winona, and bought the land at government price, a dollar and a quarter an acre.

## THE CINCINNATI SOCIETY

The beginning of 1855 there was considerable discussion regarding the enlargement of scope of the Turner societies. While this was proceeding the *Turn Zeitung*, a publication of Philadelphia, in its issue of March 29, 1855, published a communication under the heading of "practical gymnastics," which called attention of the members to the importance of a practical colonization project.

Urged by the friends of this scheme the Cincinnati Turngemeinde, on April 20, appointed a committee consisting of J. G. Herzsch, A. Tafel, A. Fischer, Nicolaus Meyer and William Pfaender, for the purpose of further considerations of the plans, a constitution, by-laws, etc., for a society. This society was for temporary purposes called the "Colonization Society of North America." The idea of this society, without being Utopian in character, had a wider scope of operation in mind than had the Chicago society. The Cincinnati Society involved the idea of obtaining means for carrying out a broad and liberal scheme of development, physical and mental, on the wide prairies of the West. It was founded when the theory of "Know-Nothingism" was at its greatest height and these people desired to cut away such barriers by settling in the far West by themselves and there build up, as it were, a little empire of their own, where narrow sectarianism could not find a home, but where freedom to all honorable people, regardless what country they chanced to be born in, might be enjoyed. The membership of the society greatly increased. The price of shares was fixed at fifteen dollars, and no one could hold more than two shares. Each shareholder was entitled to one lot on the townsite and a small area of ground outside for garden purposes, and to secure a larger tract of land at cost price for such as wished to engage in agriculture. William Pfaender, William Seeger and A. Prieser were sent out in the early spring of 1856 to look for a suitable place for such settlement. They looked through the states of Missouri, Iowa, Kansas, Nebraska and finally Minnesota. At St. Paul they were informed that there was a settlement of Germans up the Minnesota River, and they at once started for the place and found the members of the Chicago society, who as yet had not located on the site of New Ulm, but were getting ready to do so. A plat of the town had already been made.

Mr. Pfaender was acting as the agent for the Cincinnati society and liking this site, entered into negotiations for the merging of the two companies. On July 4, 1856, an agreement was effected in Chicago, the details of which were that the Chicago society should get back all the money that had been paid for land, and that the Cincinnati company should erect a warehouse and a saw-mill and flour-mill. Originally, the Chicago society gave its members twelve lots and nine acres of land outside; by the new arrangements they were to hold six lots and four acres of land outside; the Cincinnati people received three lots and four acres outside. After these plans had been agreed to Mr. Pfaender returned to New Ulm and obtained sixteen additional quarter sections of land from the government. The total amount of land acquired by purchase from the Chicago company was 4,036 acres, which included 1,700 acres laid out in the town-site. The consolidation of the two societies resulted in the formation of the "German Land Association of Minnesota," which was duly incorporated on March 4, 1857, the capital stock being named at one hundred thousand dollars, divided into shares of fifty dollars each, and in place of having to be paid for in cash, realty or personal property could be given in exchange. The society was also authorized to "erect in the counties of Brown and Nicollet, buildings, mills and other structures, with machinery for the manufacture of lumber, flour, paper, woolen goods and all such articles adapted to the wants of the country, as shall be deemed best by the stockholders." the first officers elected were William Pfaender, president; Hermann Herrendorfer, secretary; August H. Wagner, treasurer.

As soon as possible a party, under Mr. Pfaender, left in September, 1856, by steamer, from Cincinnati, which went to St. Paul. From there they made the trip in wagons to New Ulm. The names of this party were as follow: Adolph Seiter, John C. Toberer, E. Grestenhauer, William Hummell, George Guetlich, George Fein, Henry Knieff, Henry Haupt, Henry Hoffmann and William Petermann. August Schell and a few others had started on in advance of these just named. On their arrival they found a town consisting of twenty-three shanties scattered over a stretch of three miles.

In the autumn of 1856 a store was started by the company, in order to provide provisions for the settlers. It stood where later stood the Pennsylvania House. It was a two-story building of rough lumber, ten by thirty feet. William Pfaender was placed in charge; everything was sold to the settlers at actual cost.

## Immigrants of 1857

In the spring of 1857 between sixty and seventy more settlers left Cincinnati for this place. They chartered the steamer "Frank Steele" to convey them the entire distance. They started too early in the season and were tied up at Lake Pepin for quite a long time, but finally arrived at New Ulm without accident. Their coming called for more stores and shops which were at once provided. By 1860 the census reports showed that Brown County, including the village of New Ulm, had 2,339 population, and the larger part of these resided in and near the village itself. The further settlements in the county will be traced out in giving the township histories in this volume.

## Early Hardships Endured

None but those who have had a similar experience can possibly appreciate the trials and hardships endured by the pioneer settlers—men and women—who laid well the foundations of New Ulm and Brown County, Minnesota. The Chicago settlers (first colony that came to New Ulm's site), had at the time of selling a part of their possessions here, almost exhausted their means of support, and, knowing that the favorable location of their town would be without benefit to them unless they would give others a chance to settle among them, the offer of the Cincinnati gentlemen was quite readily accepted. The Chicago society consisted of some two hundred persons. They sold their rights under conditions about as follows: Each member was to receive thirty-three dollars in cash, six building lots, to be determined by chance, and one of the surveyed four-acre lots adjoining the "city."

The first settlers had already built a mill by which lumber might be sawed, and the Cincinnati colony were pledged to erect a large warehouse and erect a flouring-mill. The offer was accepted, and during the same year many of the Cincinnati society arrived—their society had a total membership of thirteen hundred.

The new addition was of great benefit to the colony; but it also brought some hardships with it, too. They consumed large amounts of provisions and it was with great difficulty that they could freight the most necessary articles in way of provisions from St. Paul, a distance of one hundred and twenty miles over bad roads and unabridged streams. The consequence of this was that provisions at New Ulm were sometimes extremely high. Many had neither money nor work and were now in great need. Corn bread was the main means of support, and having no lard, this was poorly baked. All sorts of means were resorted to, to exist at all. A man named Haeberle was obliged after planting his potatoes in the spring, to dig them up again for immediate food for his family. Many of the immigrants had no accommodations whatever. The expenses for their long journey here had deprived them of what little money they did possess before starting. Still, they felt proud and happy to see the rays of the sun fall through their windows into a room they could rightfully call their own room. Many a house had no roof, or only a part of one, and an umbrella at table or bed was at times considered a blessing indeed. Great privations, even of the absolute necessities to sustain life, were common in early days in New Ulm.

Again, for the necessaries of life they often had to pay enormous prices. A barrel of flour was sold at twenty-two dollars. (Ed. Note: According to Michael J. Variola, *Everyday Life During the Civil War: A Guide for Writers, Students and Historians*. (Cincinnati: Writer's Digest Books, 1999), flour sold for $6 per barrel in 1861, but then rose to $16 to $40 per barrel [ca. 196 pounds] in 1862 due to scarcity caused by the Civil War.). The first wheat was sown in the spring of 1856, but it was partly eaten by the blackbirds, and yielded poorly. They did not really succeed in raising much wheat until 1858. The first serious attempt at wheat growing was six miles northwest of New Ulm. Three farmers—Athanasius and Anton Henle and Benedict Drezler—had stacked their wheat at one place, in order to more easily get it threshed in the fall, after it had "gone through the sweat." This was in 1858 and they had a most excellent wheat crop and had high hopes built up for themselves and neighbors less fortunate. But alas, a prairie fire came in and swept it into ashes in an instant. On account of this, and other fires caught from this, many lost all the grain raised that season. The prices naturally went up. Potatoes were sold at three dollars a bushel, and a hen and a few chickens sold in New Ulm for five dollars. Even a cat was sold at five dollars. Mice were very numerous and it is related that one enterprising individual loaned out his cat to others for a certain time, for which he charged two dollars.

Instead of tobacco they smoked leaves and chewed roots from the nearby forests. Again, when a person chanced to have some article of home-produced provisions to spare, but few had any money with which to purchase it of the producer. This went on in the vicinity of New Ulm for five or eight years, until the country was gradually developed into a self-sustaining community.

## 42. The City of New Ulm

New Ulm, the seat of justice of Brown County, on the right bank of the Minnesota River, was named by its founders after an important city and an old fort standing on the shore of the Danube in Wurtemberg—Ulm—which word is a combination of the initials of the old Roman legend, "Ultra limites militares," which, translated into our language signifies "Beyond the military border," as the

Romans usually called the territory adjoining their possessions in distant countries. It will be understood by the readers from what has already been noted, this place in exclusively a German town, hence it was but natural that the founders named it from Ulm, in Wurtemberg, and added the prefix "New," making it New Ulm.

The object in laying out New Ulm was stated in a resolution passed by the company or colony that headed the enterprise in the following words: "the object of the German Land Company is to procure a home for every German laborer, popish priests and lawyers excepted in some healthy and productive district, located on some navigable river." With the passing years, both priest and lawyer have here found a welcome and have been numerous, as well as truly law-abiding citizens of a sprightly city whose history reads not unlike a romance from the early fifties on down for more than a third of a century, which covered the awful baptism of blood during the 1862 massacre, as well as that never-to-be forgotten summer in 1881, when the city was destroyed by a cyclone of fearful velocity.

"The German Land Association of Minnesota" was formed by act of the Legislature, March 4, 1857, by William Pfaender, president; Adolph Fischer, Fred Werner, C. Victor Bechmann, Julius Fischer, Adolph Forbeiger, Charles Stroebel, Albert Tafel, Henry Essmann, Charles Floto, Max Wocher and their associates. These parties made a second survey of the townsite and the land was entered by Judge A. G. Chatfield, at the land office at Winona.

At present the city is built up with many brick business houses and the residence districts are scarcely excelled in cities much larger than New Ulm. Excellent deposits of clay, stone and sand are found in and near the city. The railroad facilities are excellent in all directions and the wealth accumulated largely by the painstaking German and other foreign elements, has for years supported the numerous strong banking concerns, and the number of unfortunate poor in few in number.

## THE BEGINNINGS

New Ulm was platted in 1856 and in 1858 it had a newspaper known as the *New Ulm Pioneer*, the files of which show the following to have been the make-up of the village at that date: Fifty-nine hundred building lots and four hundred and ninety-three outlots; ninety buildings with six stores, a woolen mill, two blacksmiths shops, a saw- and grist-mill. Its population was then one thousand and thirty-four, with four hundred and forty voters, while the entire county only had six hundred and fifty-five voters.

The first mill in the place was the Eagle mill—a saw and grist-mill combined, erected in 1856.

The old Dakota House was opened to the public on April 16, 1859, by Seiter & Erd.

The first store was started by Adolph Seiter, just to the west of the village in 1856. The first real store or business house in New Ulm was that of F. Roebecke, who purchased the store above mentioned.

## BUSINESS OF 1916

The latest directory of the city gives these as the principal places of business: Four banks, one mortgage and loan company, five hotels, six grain elevators, a commercial club, an opera house, an armory, two extensive flouring mills, a feed-mill, a pipe-organ factory, three breweries and overall factory, bottling works, a saw-mill, a woolen-mill, brick-kilns, two hospitals, a creamery, two stone-quarry companies, four weekly newspapers (two English and two German), a produce company, a steam laundry, two express companies (Adams and American), a greenhouse, an ice company and the usual number of retail stores and shops found in cities of this class.

## THE BREWING INDUSTRY

Brewing has always been one of the leading industries in New Ulm, the first attempt being made in January, 1858, by Anton Friton, when he built the pioneer brewing establishment. In January, 1861, in the valley of the Cottonwood River, near the village of New Ulm, August Schell commenced his brewing plant and this was highly successful. In 1865, Betz & Hauenstein completed their brewery.

A distillery was started by H. A. Subilia and was ready for business on April 6, 1861. It stood just under the bluff, a little to the north of the street leading from the city to the present college grounds, near the Hermann monument. The old brick smoke-stack is all that remains as the monument of that early still, where unadulterated spirits were produced and sold in the markets of the country.

The New Ulm Brewing and Malting Company was established in 1910, as the company is now formed. The incorporation officers are now: President, John Schneider; vice-president, Herman Nogel; secretary, Joseph F. Groebner; treasurer, Otto Meyer. The authorized capital is fifty thousand dollars. Twelve men are employed, and large amounts of grain are annually used in the establishment. Minnesota and Iowa take a greater part of the output from this brewing concern. The capacity is ten thousand barrels per year, but on account of the recent temperance agitation and war upon the part of the "Drys" the limit is not quite reached of late.

This brewing plant is the direct successor to the first brewery in New Ulm—Anton Friton's—established in 1858, near the Minneapolis & St. Louis depot, and the Park of today. Mr. Friton was succeeded by Joseph Schumaker and he was succeeded by the present owners.

The Schell Brewing Company was established at New Ulm in 1861, under its present name. August Schell was the proprietor. It is now operated under a stock company capital, including the heirs of the late Anton Schell. The officers of the company are George Marti, president; August A. Schneider, vice-president; E. A. Habberg, secretary and treasurer. The plant's capacity is now eighteen thousand barrels annually; the grain consumed is about twenty thousand bushels. The product is sold in Minnesota and Iowa and the company enjoys an excellent mail order business. The capital is three hundred thousand dollars; number of men employed, thirty-two. The grounds surrounding the plant are indeed beautiful—a real park in which twelve deer are kept.

The Hauenstein Brewing Company, at New Ulm was established in 1864 by John Hauenstein. The present officers of the corporation are: Charles Hauenstein, president; Mrs. Henrietta Hauenstein, treasurer; John

Hauenstein, Jr.; Martin Hose, secretary. The capacity of the plant is twenty thousand barrels, and they consume about thirty-five bushels of grain per annum. The product of this brewing company finds sale mostly in Minnesota, North and South Dakota and originally in Iowa. An extensive mail-order business is also transacted. Forty men are constantly employed. The capital under which this concern is operated is one hundred thousand dollars.

### FLOURING INDUSTRY

Brown County has long since been noted for its flour-making industry. The census in 1905 says this county made more flour than any county in Minnesota, outside of Hennepin (Minneapolis). In 1908 the daily grind in the various mills amounted to thirteen thousand barrels at New Ulm, Sleepy Eye and Springfield. The capital then invested was one million, eight hundred and thirty-nine dollars.

The Eagle Mills, at New Ulm, are successors to the old pioneer mill. This was rebuilt by Beinhorn and Rethfeld after the Indian massacre in 1862, when it was burned. In 1865 it was doing a flourishing business; its capacity was fifty barrels per day. It was a combined saw- and grist-mill until 1874. In 1880 it was converted into a "full roller process" mill, making two hundred barrels per day; in 1897 it was increased to a seven-hundred barrel mill—then later to a thousand barrels daily. In 1898 it was enlarged into a two-thousand-five-hundred-barrel mill. In 1899 the company built two elevators and now employ three hundred people in the mills and elevators the company owns throughout the Dakotas and Minnesota. About one-half are employed in the mills, proper. In 1908 this mill was running under the capacity of five thousand barrels daily; had three immense grain elevators in New Ulm, with a capacity of four hundred thousand bushels of wheat. They also had fifty-one grain elevators scattered throughout Dakota and Minnesota. Their plant is connected with both the Minneapolis & St. Louis and Northwestern railway systems. "Gold coin" is one of the brands of flour that has made these mills famous from coast to coast. They have offices in Chicago, Philadelphia and New York, also have representatives in London; also sell in Holland and other European countries. These mills grind approximately five million bushels of grain annually. Their expense is about a half million dollars a year. By all odds it is the greatest flour producing plant in southern Minnesota.

Charles Silverson, a former president of the company owning these mills, had been a leading figure in the management and expansion of this great flour industry. He died in September, 1912, after several years' illness.

The Cottonwood roller mills, near the city of New Ulm, are the property of John Bentzin. These mills were established in 1878 and have a daily capacity of one hundred barrels. It is the last custom mill left in the country, from the numerous ones it once had. Here excellent flour, both wheat and rye, as well as corn meal and graham flour are produced for customers living in the surrounding country.

## The Overall Factory

Johnson Company, of St. Peter, have a branch factory in New Ulm in which they make men's overalls extensively. They employ fifty-five persons, of whom fifty-three are women. The weekly output is two hundred and eighty dozen. This branch factory was established in New Ulm in 1910 and does an extensive business. The present manager is Charles Lindeman, Jr.

## The Stone Industry

One of the paying industries of New Ulm of recent years has been that of getting out crushed stone, for paving, concrete work an general highway building. There are two incorporated concerns that operate extensive quarries near the city limits to the southeast. The quarries are both situated just across the Minnesota River, in Nicollet County, but the owners of both plants are local people for the most part, and have offices in New Ulm.

As early as 1888 the New Ulm Stone Company was incorporated and for many years quarried the granite for building purposes, but in 1905 they put in operation stone crushing mills, of which they now operate three, and have a capacity of about four carloads a day. Most of the output of this quarry goes to points in Iowa—Mason City, Sioux City, Storm Lake, etc., where it is used in street work largely. Thirty men are employed in the working season, and these are local men and the payroll is appreciated by the retail dealers of the city. Years ago much of the product of these quarries was used in the Twin Cities. The capital stock is same as when incorporated—twenty-five thousand dollars. The first set of promoters—the incorporators, were: Jacob Pfenningier, W. Boersch,

August Schell and George G. Benz. They own a quarter section of land which contains an inexhaustible supply of fine granite. The company also ships immense amounts of sand and gravel to distant points.

The other company engaged in a similar business is the Jasper Granite Company, who operates on forty acres of leased land, near the company's holdings just named above. This was originally worked by the Minnesota Flint Company and about 1908 put in crushers also. Local and Minneapolis capital is invested in this enterprise. Mr. Wycoff is the manager of this company and has offices in the Olsen block. The New Ulm Stone Company has for its president and manager, H. Held, who successfully cares for the large shipments of stone, sand and gravel.

### The Ice Business

The only company engaged in handling ice at New Ulm is the New Ulm Ice Company, composed of Herman Held and E. H. Haeberle, who put up large amounts of ice from the Minnesota River. They have extensive ice warehouses and ship much ice to distant points, besides handling the local trade and that of the Minneapolis & St. Louis Railroad Company. They usually ship a hundred and fifty cars of ice in the season. They handle refrigerators and contract for building sand, gravel and crushed stone. Many of the men who work in the stone quarries also assist this company in the ice harvest.

### Municipal History

New Ulm was incorporated in March, 1857, and William Pfaender was elected its first president. Later it was incorporated as a borough, with Charles Roos as mayor. A city charter was granted New Ulm on February 24, 1876, with Charles Roos as mayor and Jacob Nix as clerk. Since the place was incorporated into a city the records are all intact, but on account of the Indian depredations during the massacre in August, 1862, the early village records were all destroyed or lost. From 1862 on a record showing the chairman and mayors of the place is as follow: F. Gommell, chairman. 1862-63; R. Fischer, chairman, 1863-64; John Hauenstein, chairman. 1864-65; R. Forster, chairman, 1865-66; L. Naegele, chairman, 1866-68; Dr. A. Mueller, chairman, 1868-69 and 1870. The place then became an incorporated borough with Charles Roos as mayor; the councilmen were then, F. Forster, Dr. C. Weschcke, H. Loheyde; clerk, E. A. Hausman;

treasurer, William Guetling; assessor, E. A. Hausman; justice of the peace, L. Bogen; marshal, F. Gommell; attorney. E. St. Julien Cox.

Since then the mayors have been: Charles Roos, 1872-73; William Pfaender, 1874-76; Charles Roos, 1876-78; C. Weschcke, 1878-82; John C. Rudolph, 1882-83; H. B. Contans, 1883-86; C. Weschcke, 1886-88; John C. Rudolph, 1888-89; Charles Wagner, 1889-93; E. G. Koch, 1893-96; C. Weschcke, 1896-98; Jacob Klossner (acting mayor) 1899; C. Weschcke, 1899-1904; Charles Silverson, 1904-09; Joseph Bobleter, 1910; John P. Graff, 1910-12; Dr. L. A. Fritsche, 1912-16, and still serving as mayor of the city.

The officers for 1916 are as follow: Mayor, Dr. L. A. Fritsche; city clerk, William Backer; treasurer, Gottlieb Oswald; city attorney, Alb Pfaender; city engineer, F. D. Minium; superintendent of water and lights, A. J. Mueller; city council, Fred Behnke, president; Fred Hamann, Wm. Eibner, Emil Mueller, L. B. Krook and Christ Filzen, Jr.

The city's finances in 1916 are as follow: electric light bonds out, $30,000; sewer bonds out, $10,000; new state loan, $40,000; state loan, $25,000. total, $105,000.

The water plant consists of three wells, the depth of which is—one is 186 feet; one 183 feet, and one 364 feet deep. Water is pumped from the lighting plant to the reservoir on Hermann's Heights, west of the city, and this basin holds, together with the lesser one at the foot of the hill by the pumping plant, a total of one million and ninety thousand gallons.

The electric light plant was formerly a private concern, but in April, 1901, was taken over by the city, and bonds were then voted to the amount of twenty thousand dollars. In all the plant has cost the city thirty thousand dollars.

The city has only five blocks of real paving which consists of an excellent quality of creosote block paving on Minnesota Street, placed there in 1914.

The present police force is three men. A volunteer fire company of forty-five competent men keep safe the city from fire ravages. They are aided by the direct pressure from the water-works and an engine. The only building owned by the city is the one-story brick, situated at 109 North

Broadway, in which the clerk holds his office, and there the city council meets, as does the fire company.

There are now one hundred and twenty-two fire plugs and twelve miles of water main.

## COMMERCIAL CLUB

The business interests of New Ulm have been greatly advanced of recent years by the re-organization of the old Commercial Club. This club maintains fine rooms on Minnesota Avenue; have more than two hundred "live wire" members, who see that nothing is lost sight of in promoting the city's best interests. They work for Brown County, as well as for the city. They have already aided in bringing much new business to the place. The membership is composed of the best men in New Ulm.

## Editor's Conclusion

As an historian of New Ulm and environs, Dr. Fritsche in 1916 aimed to document and record the 1862 Uprising within the framework of his Brown County history, and did so by collecting eyewitness accounts, historical recollections, and assessments of the conflict. The history notes that the "honest debt contracted by the government, was, with the exception of an insignificant portion of it, never paid; and this was the principal cause of the dissatisfaction and revolt of the Indians." Also, "the government did, indeed, pay the stipulated sum regularly, but the superintendents, agents, etc., to whom the money was entrusted for distribution and payment, managed to keep the greater portion of it for themselves."

Moreover, "The Indians were often so much cheated that they had as little pay after a payment which would amount to hundreds of thousands of dollars, as they had before." Fritsche cites Bishop Whipple's observation that "there is not a man in America, who ever gave an hour's reflection to the subject, who does not know that our Indian system is an organized system of robbery and has been for years a disgrace to the nation." Dr. Fritsche, therefore, places the blame for the Uprising squarely on the shoulders of the government's Indian policy and system, and strongly condemns it for being the ultimate cause of the conflict that ensued.

Although clearly identifying the governmental Indian policy and its administration as the cause of the Uprising, and soundly condemning this corrupt and unjust system, Dr. Fritsche supports the punishment meted to the leaders of the Uprising, whom he describes as "these merciless outlaws who had shed the blood of innocent women and children in the time of peace." He writes that "the voice of the blood of innocence crying from the ground, the wailings of mothers bereft of their children were hushed in the tender cry of sympathy for the condemned." He thereby calls attention to the fact that close to a thousand people were killed during the Uprising, and that this should not be overlooked.

Fritsche also refers to the "trend of sentiment in Minnesota at that time" in support of the punishment that took place after the Uprising. This places his position within the broader context of public support across the state for punishment. He, therefore, condemns the wrongs and injustices committed against the Sioux, but finds the death and destruction that followed without justification, and worthy of punishment. In short, he finds no justification for what he views as crimes against humanity.

Fritsche's work answers the basic question of how those who survived the Uprising viewed it, its causes, and its aftermath. His work amounts to what is probably the most comprehensive documentary history by a German-American author. It should also be remembered that Fritsche was the son of a German immigrant family that had survived the conflict, and that his work should be viewed more as a primary, rather than a secondary source, as it contains many first-hand accounts.

Regarding the language of the history, it should be noted that as a documentary history this reflects the spirit of the time. The anti-Indian bias of the eyewitnesses and the history in general is readily apparent. Such views typify not only those who survived the war, but were likely fairly widespread at the time. It should be recalled that the Uprising took place fourteen years prior to the Battle at the Little Bighorn, which led to the demise of Custer and his troops, and called forth even more negative rhetoric and hostility from the public at large. The Sioux accordingly are viewed here by the survivors of the conflict as savages and the settlers as the bearers of civilization. For example, in the biographical introduction to Dr. Fritsche, it is stated that he witnessed the transformation and "the reclamation of the wilderness...from the idle and indolent savage."

Even Bishop Whipple, the chief opponent of the government's Indian policy, writes that this policy was responsible for "dragging the savage down to a brutishness unknown to his fathers..." Hence, even those supportive of the Sioux subscribe to a view of the Native American of at best a "noble savage." Such views are reflected in this documentary history.

In conclusion, this work provides us with access to a documentary history assembled by a German-American whose family experienced and survived the 1862 conflict. As such, it provides insight into their perspective. Hopefully, this documentary history will fill a gap in the literature on the topic, and contribute to further research and study.

# Index

| | |
|---|---|
| Aeche-ga (To Grow Upon) | 112 |
| Aherin, Matthew | 121 |
| Albrecht, H. | 79 |
| Almond | 51 |
| Am-da-cha (Broken to Pieces) | 110 |
| Anderson, Mary | 112 |
| Ange, Hypolite | 111 |
| Assal | 164 |
| Austin, Horace | 94 |
| Ayers, Dr. | 52, 89, 93-96 |
| Backer, William | 183 |
| Baker, Howard | 36 |
| Baker, Mrs. | 36, 37 |
| Baker, Robert | 135 |
| Baptiste | 115 |
| Barth, G. W. Otto | 121 |
| Bechmann, Victor | 177 |
| Behnke, Adam | 170 |
| Behnke, Fred | 183 |
| Behnke, Henry | 45 |
| Beinhorn, Frederick | 163, 164, 170, 180 |
| Bellm, John | 12, 48 |
| Bentzin, John | 181 |
| Benz, George G. | 182 |
| Berghold, Alexander | vii, 21 |
| Betz | 179 |
| Beussman, H. H. | 16 |
| Bierbauer, William | 14, 52, 89, 93 |
| Bishop, John F. | 144-147 |

Blatz, Albert ................................................... 170
Blatz, Valentine ................................................ 170
Blodgett, William ............................................... 148
Boardmann, Sheriff .............................................. 48
Bobleter, Joseph ........................................... 6, 56, 183
Bobleter, Maria Hartman- ........................................ 83
Boeringen ...................................................... 167
Boersch, W. .................................................... 181
Brandt, J. ..................................................... 167
Brant, Charles S. ............................................... 135
Brennan ........................................................ 147
Brockman, H. ................................................... 47
Brown, Major ................................................... 115
Brunner, Vincent ................................................ 66
Bryan, William Jennings ...................................... 7, 87
Buell, Major ................................................... 89
Bureau ......................................................... 155
Burgess, Margaret ............................................... 89
Burgess, Nehemiah S. ........................................ 88, 89
Burk, Captain .................................................. 115
Burt, Captain .................................................. 109
Bushe .......................................................... viii
Campbell, Baptiste ............................................. 111
Carroll ..................................................... 48, 51
Carroll, William ............................................... 121
Casimer ........................................................ 43
Castor ......................................................... 57
Castor, Jacob .................................................. 121
Chan-ka-hda (Near the Woods) ................................... 112
Chas-ka-dan (the First Born if a Son) .......................... 111
Chaska ......................................................... 146

| | |
|---|---|
| Chatfield, A. G. | 177 |
| Chay-tan-hoon-ka (The Parent Hawk) | 112 |
| Chief Red Iron, Ma-zas-ha | 27, 28 |
| Chittendon, R. H. | 139 |
| Cockburn, John A. | 7 |
| Coffin, Samuel | 93 |
| Conrad, C. M. | 133 |
| Contans, H. B. | 183 |
| Coon | 48 |
| Cox, Julien | 16, 17, 55, 58, 99, 183 |
| Culver, Charles M. | 141 |
| Culver, Lieutenant | 31, 135 |
| Custer | 109 |
| Dambach, Joseph | 66, 167, 168, 170 |
| Dana, Napoleon Jackson Tecumseh | 133, 134 |
| Daniels, Asa W. | 121 |
| Daniels, Dr. | 52, 89 |
| Dederich, A. | 170 |
| Detrich | 76 |
| Dickinson, J. C. | 141 |
| Diederich, A. | 40 |
| Diepolder, Fidel | 11 |
| Divoll | 110 |
| Do-wan-za (The Singer) | 110 |
| Dodd, Captain | 57, 91-94, 97, 98 |
| Dodd, William B. | 121 |
| Drexler, Benedict | 81, 167 |
| Drezler | 75 |
| Drezler, Benedict | 125, 174 |
| Drezler, Frank | 125 |
| Duhrssen, Alfred | 5 |

Duly, William J. ............................................. 115
Dunn ........................................................ 147
Dunn, James ................................................ 144
E-tay-doo-ta (Red Face) .................................... 110
Eberhart, A. O. .............................................. 6
Eggensdoefer, Theresia ..................................... 125
Eibner, Wm. ................................................ 183
Emmerich, Joseph .......................................... 125
England, William ........................................... 121
Ensderle, Ludwig ........................................... 170
Erd ................................................ 46, 48, 57, 178
Essmann, Henry ............................................ 177
Faribault .................................................... 155
Faribault, David ............................................ 110
Fein, George ................................................ 172
Fenske, Julius .......................................... 40, 76
Filzen, Christ, Jr. ........................................... 183
Fin, Martin ................................................. 82
Finch, Doctor .............................................. 115
Fink, Elizabeth ............................................. 66
Fink, M. .................................................... 75
Fink, Martin ............................................ 82, 125
Fink, Max ............................................... 82, 125
Fink, Monica ............................................ 82, 125
Finke, Elise ................................................ 167
Fischer, A. ............................................ 171, 177
Fischer, Max ............................................... 177
Fischer, R. ................................................. 182
Flandrau, Charles E. ...... 14, 45, 52, 55, 56, 89, 92-94, 96, 99, 122, 135, 170
Fletcher, Duncan ............................................ 7
Floto, Charles .............................................. 177

Forbeiger, Adolph ............................................. 177
Forster, F. .................................................. 182
Forster, R. .................................................. 182
Foster ...................................................... 46
Frass, John .............................................. viii, ix
Frazir, Jack ................................................ 137
Friton, Anton ......................................... 178, 179
Fritsche ..................................................... 4
Fritsche, Albert ............................................... 9
Fritsche, Alexander Frederick .................................. 9
Fritsche, Amalie .............................................. 9
Fritsche, Bertha .............................................. 4
Fritsche, Carl J. ............................................ 4, 9
Fritsche, Elsa ................................................ 9
Fritsche, Fred W. ............................................. 4
Fritsche, Frederick ................................ 3, 4, 11, 12
Fritsche, Henry W. ............................................ 4
Fritsche, John Karl ........................................... 3
Fritsche, Louis Albert ............... v-vii, ix, 3-5, 7-9, 183, 185, 186
Fritsche, Louise .............................................. 9
Fritsche, Otto A. ............................................. 4
Fritsche, Rudolph E. .......................................... 4
Fritsche, Theodore ......................................... vii, 9
Fritsche, William ............................................. 9
Galbraith, Agent ............................................. 31
Galbraith, Major ............................................. 91
Garvie ..................................................... 111
Gere, T. P. ................................................. 142
Gluth, August ............................................... 161
Gommell, F. ........................................... 182, 183
Goode, William ............................................. 135

Gorman, Lt. .................................................... 135
Graff, John P. .................................................. 183
Grear, Mark M. ................................................. 135
Grestenhauer, E. ................................................ 172
Groebner, Joseph F. ............................................. 179
Gross .......................................................... 96
Guetlich, George ............................................... 172
Guetling, Julius ............................................ 12, 13
Guetling, William .............................................. 183
Guth, Fred ..................................................... 125
Ha-pan (Second Child) .......................................... 110
Ha-pin-kpa (The Tip of the Horn) ............................... 111
Haack, Max ..................................................... 121
Haag, Christ ................................................... 125
Haag, Christian ............................................. 43, 75
Habberg, E. A. ................................................. 179
Haeberle ........................................ 56, 165, 167, 174
Haeberle, E. H. ................................................ 182
Haeberle, Jacob ................................................ 121
Hamann, Fred ................................................... 183
Hammer ......................................................... 56
Hartman, Florian ........................... 43, 75, 82, 83, 125
Hartman-Bobleter, Maria ........................................ 83
Hartneck ....................................................... 56
Hartneck, J. ................................................... 56
Hauenstein .................................................... 179
Hauenstein, Charles ........................................... 179
Hauenstein, Henrietta ......................................... 179
Hauenstein, John .......................................... 12, 179
Hauenstein, John Jr. ...................................... 180, 182
Haupt .......................................................... 40

| | |
|---|---|
| Haupt, Henry | 172 |
| Hausman, E. A. | 182, 183 |
| Hay-pe-dan (The Third Child) | 110 |
| Hayden, John | 154 |
| Hayden, Mike | 154 |
| Held | 56 |
| Held, Herman | 182 |
| Hellmann, August | 12 |
| Henkle, Mary | 125 |
| Henle, Anton | 66, 75-77, 81, 82, 85, 123, 174 |
| Henle, Athanasius | 11, 40, 41, 61, 66, 75, 76, 79, 82, 123, 164-167, 169, 174 |
| Henle, Martin | 77-79, 82 |
| Henle, Mary | 82 |
| Henle, Theresa | 75, 81 |
| Hermann, L. | 167 |
| Herrendorfer, Hermann | 172 |
| Herrick | 7 |
| Herriott, Mayor | 8 |
| Herzsch, J. G. | 171 |
| Heyers, Carl | 125 |
| Heyers, Dorothea | 125 |
| Heyers, Henry | 125 |
| Heyers, Joachim | 125 |
| Heyers, John | 125 |
| Hin-han-shoon-ko-yag-ma-ne (Walks Clothed with an Owl's Tail) | 109 |
| Hinman, J. D. | 143-145 |
| Hinton | 51 |
| Hitz, Paul | 170 |
| Ho-tan-in-koo (Voice That Appears Coming) | 112 |
| Hoffmann, Henry | 172 |
| Hose, Martin | 180 |

Houghton, Newell E. .............................................. 121
Huey, William .................................. 15, 16, 55, 96, 97, 99
Huggins, Amos W. ............................................... 111
Huggins, Rufus .......................................... 100, 121
Hummell, William ............................................... 172
Hummelscheim ................................................... 164
Humphry, Doctor ................................................. 92
Hunter, Alexander ............................................... 109
Hunter, Mrs. .................................................... 110
Hutchinson, William B. .......................................... 147
Ives ............................................................. 48
Jinton ........................................................... 48
Johnson, John A. ............................................... 6, 7
Jones ........................................................... 140
Jones, Judson ................................................. 88, 89
Jones, R. ..................................................... 36, 37
Jones, Sergeant .......................... 14, 135, 136, 139, 140
Julius .......................................................... 167
Juni, Benedict .................................................. 153
Kahlfeld ........................................................ 56
Kaus, Anton .................................................... 163
Keck, John ..................................................... 125
Kiessling ................................................. 164, 170
Kintore, Earl of ................................................. 7
Kirby ........................................................... 48
Kirschstein, Julius .............................................. 121
Kitzmann, Louis ................................................. 161
Kleinknecht .................................................... 167
Klossner, Jacob ................................................. 183
Knieff, Henry .................................................. 172
Koch, E. G. .................................................... 183

| | |
|---|---|
| Kock | 167 |
| Kraemer | 167 |
| Krause, Ferdinand | 121 |
| Krook, L. B. | 183 |
| Kropper, P. | 12 |
| Kulp, Washington | 121 |
| Kumrows | 155 |
| La Framboise, Joseph | 65, 133, 166-169 |
| LaFramboise, Joseph | 164 |
| Lamb | 48, 51 |
| Lamb, George | 121 |
| Le Butt | 111 |
| Lean Bear | 27 |
| Lee, Thomas | 133 |
| Lemmon | 48 |
| Lemon, DeWitt | 121 |
| Lillie, Christian | 3 |
| Lillie, Louise | 4 |
| Lind, John | 6 |
| Lindeman, Charles, Jr. | 181 |
| Little Crow | viii, 55, 91, 136, 139, 144, 146 |
| Loheyde, H. | 182 |
| Loomis | 48, 51 |
| Loomis, A. D. | 121 |
| Loomis, Uri | 121 |
| Lump, Mathias | 11 |
| Ma-hoo-way-wa (He Comes for Me) | 112 |
| Ma-ka-ta-e-ne-jin (One Who Stands on the Earth) | 111 |
| Ma-za-boon-doo (Iron Blower) | 110 |
| Mack | 167, 168 |
| Mack, Peter | 66 |

Mah-pe-o-ke-ne-jin (Who Stands on the Cloud) ..................... 111
Mahpya Wicasta (Man-of-the-Cloud) ............................... 22
Maloney, William ............................................... 121
Manager ....................................................... 156
Marsh, Captain ..................... 95, 110, 134, 140-148, 155, 157, 158
Marshall, Colonel .............................................. 115
Marti, George .................................................. 179
Massapust .............................................. 41, 165, 167
Massapust, Fr. ................................................. 166
Massapust, Frank ............................................... 125
Massapust, Franz ............................................. 66, 75
Massapust, Frederick ........................................... 164
Massapust, Johann ............................................... 72
Massapust, Johann Jr. ........................................ 72, 77
Massapust, Julia ............................................ 72, 125
Massapust, Maria ................................................ 72
Massapust, Mary ................................................ 125
Massapust, Mary Ann ............................................ 125
May, Barbara ................................................... 125
May, Bertha .................................................... 125
May, Henry ..................................................... 125
May, Sebastian ................................................. 125
Mayo, Dr. ...................................... 52, 89, 93, 95, 96, 98
McCole, Edward ................................................. 163
McGrew, Sergeant ........................................... 31, 136
McMahon, Dr. ......................................... 52, 89, 96
McPhail, Samuel ................................................ 139
Meagher, John F. ............................................... 121
Meierding, H. .................................................. 170
Merkle, Carl ................................................... 125
Merkle, Martin .................................................. 82

| | |
|---|---|
| Merriam, Governor | 122 |
| Messerschmidt | 164 |
| Messmer, Anton | 125 |
| Messmer, Joseph | 125 |
| Messmer, Mary Ann | 125 |
| Messner, Joseph | 40 |
| Metzke, Frederick | 164 |
| Meyer, Ludwig | 66, 164, 166, 167, 170 |
| Meyer, Matthias | 121 |
| Meyer, Nicolaus | 171 |
| Meyer, Otto | 179 |
| Meyerding, Henry | 170 |
| Michelowski | 56 |
| Miles, Mail-carrier | 32 |
| Milord, Henry | 111 |
| Minium, F. D. | 183 |
| Mueller, Dr. Alfred | 140, 164, 182, 183 |
| Mueller, Dr. Eliza | 134, 140 |
| Mueller, Emil | 183 |
| Mueller, Henry | 15 |
| Mueller, William H. | 4 |
| Myrick | 33 |
| Naegele, L. | 182 |
| Nicholson, William | 121 |
| Nightingale, Florence | 140 |
| Nix, Jacob | vii, 12-14, 44, 45, 47, 48, 55, 58, 182 |
| No-Pay-Skin (One Who Does Not Flee) | 111 |
| Nogel, Herman | 179 |
| Northrup, Anson | 139 |
| Nouse, George A. | 106 |
| O-ya-tay-a-koo (The Coming People) | 112 |

Ochs .................................................................. 43
Ochs, Anton ........................................................... 79
Ochs, Cecilia ......................................................... 43
Olson, Ole ........................................................... 121
Oswald, Gottlieb ..................................................... 183
Page, Ambassador ...................................................... 7
Palmer, Alois ............................... 11, 66, 75, 164, 166, 167
Patwell ................................................ 109, 110, 112
Pauli ................................................................. 12
Pauly ................................................................. 48
Paw Skaw (whitehead) ................................................ 159
Paza-koo-tay-wa-ne (One Who Walks Prepared to Shoot) ............... 111
Peel, Viscount ........................................................ 7
Peller, John ..................................................... 12, 13
Pelzel, Brigitta ..................................................... 125
Pelzl, Carl ...................................................... 43, 75
Petermann, William ................................................... 172
Pfaender, Albert ............................................... 123, 183
Pfaender, Amalie ...................................................... 9
Pfaender, William ............ 9, 44, 61, 121, 163, 171, 172, 177, 182, 183
Pfeiffer ............................................................. 164
Pfenningier, Jacob ................................................... 181
Potter, Captain ....................................................... 87
Pouser, Frederick ..................................................... 48
Prieser, A. .......................................................... 171
Pritchette, Kitzing ................................................... 21
Quane, Jerry ..................................................... 99, 121
Quinn ...................................................... 141, 145, 146
Ramsey, Alexander ................................................ 23, 27
Ramsey, Gov. ......................................................... 137
Randall ............................................................... 25

Randall, R. H. .................................................. 138
Rda-in-yan-ka (Rattling Rounder) ................................ 110
Red Iron's ..................................................... 28
Reeves, Gen. ................................................... 6
Rehfeld, Fred .................................................. 12
Reim, Theodore ................................................. 14
Reimans, August ................................................ 121
Reiner ......................................................... 75
Rhoner ......................................................... 83
Ridgely, Randolph .............................................. 133
Riemer, August ................................................. 12
Riggs, Rev. .................................................... 115
Roebecke, F. ................................................... 178
Roepke ......................................................... 58
Roepke, August ................................................. 121
Roessr, Barbara ................................................ 125
Roessr, George ................................................. 125
Rohner ......................................................... 43
Rohner, Barbara ................................................ 125
Rohner, John ................................................... 83, 125
Roos, Charles .................................................. 45, 76, 79, 182, 183
Rotherham, Lord ................................................ 7
Rudolph ........................................................ 44
Rudolph, John C. ............................................... 183
Rutenberg, August .............................................. 15
Rwa-ma-ne (Tinkling Water) ..................................... 110
Ryan ........................................................... 51
Saunders, E. C. ................................................ 14, 100
Schalk ......................................................... 12
Schell, Anton .................................................. 179
Schell, August ................................................. 172, 178, 179, 182

Schilling, Adolph ........................................... 15, 76, 125
Schmitz, John B. ................................................ 31, 57
Schneider, August A. ............................................... 179
Schneider, John .............................................. 40, 179
Schwandt .......................................................... vii, ix
Schwandt, Christina .................................................. ix
Schwandt, Frederick .................................................. ix
Schwandt, Karoline ................................................... ix
Schwandt, Mary .................................................... viii
Schwartz ............................................................ 167
Schwarz ............................................................. 164
Schwerdtfeger ........................................................ 45
Scott, Winfield ..................................................... 133
Seeger, William ..................................................... 171
Seeler, Charles ...................................................... 32
Seignorette, Doctor ................................................. 115
Seiter, Adolph .................................................. 172, 178
Senzke, Leopold .................................................... 121
Shakopee, Chief ..................................................... 39
Shas-ka ....................................................... 112, 113
Sheehan, Lt. ........................................................ 135
Shillock, D. G. ...................................................... 88
Shoemaker ........................................................... 98
Shoon-ka-ska (White Dog) ........................................... 110
Sibley, General ............... 17, 91, 99, 100, 121, 133, 137, 139, 140, 160
Silverson, Charles .............................................. 181, 183
Smith, Luke ........................................................ 121
Sneider ............................................................. 76
Spelbrink, Christopher .............................................. 65
Spelbrink, Louis ................................................... 123
Spenner ........................................................ 47, 48

| | |
|---|---|
| Staus, C. | 170 |
| Steinhauser, Albert | 12, 123 |
| Steinle | 40 |
| Stocker, Caroline (Zicher) | 43, 72, 125 |
| Stocker, Joseph | 43, 72 |
| Stroebel, Charles | 177 |
| Sulzdorf | 7 |
| Summers | 16, 100 |
| Summers, John | 121 |
| Sunrisen, Father | 98 |
| Sutherland, William A. | 148-150 |
| Svendson | 147 |
| Swift | 47 |
| Swift, Henry A. | 94 |
| Ta-tay-ka-gay (Wind Maker) | 111 |
| Tafel, A. | 171, 177 |
| Tag-ma-na | 22 |
| The-he-hdo-ne-cha (One Who Forbids His House) | 109 |
| Theobald | 56 |
| Thiele | 167 |
| Thieler, Mrs. | 110 |
| Thomas | 48, 51 |
| To-tay-hde-dan (Wind Comes Home) | 111 |
| To-zoo, alias Plan-doo-ta (Red Otter) | 109 |
| Toberer, John C. | 172 |
| Toon-kan-e-chah-tah-ma-ne (One Who Walks by His Grandfather) | 110 |
| Toon-kan-ko-yag-ena-gin (One Who Stands Clothed with His Grandfather) | 111 |
| Tormon, Jan | 121 |
| Tousley, Captain | 93, 95 |
| Trogdon, J. B. | 87, 88 |
| Tuttle | 48, 49 |

| | |
|---|---|
| Tuttle, Barbara | 66 |
| Tuttle, William | 121 |
| Tyler, Hugh | 23 |
| Van Buren | 147 |
| Vanosse, Joseph | 138 |
| Variola, Michael J. | 174 |
| Voehringer | 164 |
| Wa-he-kna (meaning unknown) | 110 |
| Wa-kan-tan-ka (Great Spirit) | 111 |
| Wa-kin-yan-ne (Little Thunder) | 112 |
| Wa-she-choon (Frenchman) | 111 |
| Wagner, August | 71, 172 |
| Wagner, Charles | 12, 183 |
| Wah-pe-yah-we-tah | 35 |
| Wall, M. | 66, 167 |
| Wall, O. G. | 140 |
| Walser | 165, 167 |
| Wan-pa-do-ta (Red Leaf) | 110 |
| Webster | 36 |
| Weddendorf | 46, 56 |
| Weiss | 164, 167 |
| Wellner, Henry | 15 |
| Werner, Fred | 177 |
| Weschcke, C. | 183 |
| Weschcke, Dr. | 52, 183 |
| Weschke, Mayor | 6 |
| Westphal, August | 12, 13 |
| Whipple, Bishop | 98, 127, 185, 186 |
| Whipple, J. C. | 136, 138 |
| Whitcomb, Captain | 37 |
| White Dog | 110, 143, 145, 146 |

| | |
|---|---|
| Wiedmann | 167 |
| Wilkinson, Senator | 105 |
| Williams, Miss | 110 |
| Williams, Missionary | 119 |
| Winklemann, W. | 167 |
| Wocher, Max | 177 |
| Wolff, Julius | 5 |
| Woods, Samuel | 134 |
| Wright, A. W. | 6 |
| Wy-a-tah-ta-wa (His People) | 109 |
| Wycoff | 182 |
| Young, Antoine | 111 |
| Young, Dorothy | ix |
| Young, Judge | 23 |
| Zagrotzky, Victor | 77, 79 |
| Zecher, Anton | 56 |
| Zeller | 79 |
| Zeller, Conrad | 43, 77, 82, 125 |
| Zeller, John | 125 |
| Zeller, Lucretia | 125 |
| Zeller, Martin | 125 |
| Zeller, Max | 75, 82, 125 |
| Zeller, Monika | 125 |
| Zettel, Barbara | 82, 125 |
| Zettel, Elizabeth | 125 |
| Zettel, John | 66, 75, 82, 125, 167, 169, 170 |
| Zettel, Mrs. | 75, 79 |
| Zicher, Caroline Stocker | 43 |
| Zieher | 56 |
| Zimmerman | 154 |
| Zimmerman, Gottfried | 156 |

Zimmerman, John .......................................... 156
Zollner, Xavier ............................................. 14

www.ingramcontent.com/pod-product-compliance
Lightning Source LLC
Chambersburg PA
CBHW070740160426
43192CB00009B/1518